FR. DWIGHT LONGENECKER

# An Answer, *Not* An Argument

### Essays on Apologetics

Edited by Kenneth P. Woodington

Preface by Patrick Madrid

**STAUFFER**
BOOKS

Copyright © 2019 Dwight Longenecker

All rights reserved. This publication may not be reproduced, stored in a retrieval system or transmitted in any form or by any means, electronic, mechanical, photocopying, recording or otherwise, without the prior written permission of the author.

STAUFFER BOOKS
Terra Lane, Greenville, SC

Printed by CreateSpace.

ISBN 978-0-9862713-3-5

# Contents

| | |
|---|---|
| 4 | PREFACE |
| 6 | INTRODUCTION |
| 6 | Knocking on the Door of the Grand, Old Mansion |
| 10 | WHO SAYS SO? |
| 10 | More Christianity: Affirming Not Denying |
| 15 | How Do We Know It's the True Church? |
| 23 | What is Truth? |
| 34 | Being One, Holy, Catholic and Apostolic |
| 45 | PETER AND THE PAPACY |
| 45 | Biblical Support for the Papacy |
| 54 | Come Rock! Come Rope! |
| 65 | *The Trail of Blood* and the Early Papacy |
| 75 | THE FIRST CHRISTIANS |
| 75 | How Do We Know the Gospels Are Historical? |
| 80 | A Catholic Dating Service |
| 87 | Paganism, Prophecies and Propaganda |
| 94 | The Problems with Primitivism |
| 101 | SACRAMENTS AND SALVATION |
| 101 | One Saving Action |
| 119 | Baptism Now Saves You |
| 126 | What Do We Mean by the Real Presence? |
| 134 | HOW DO YOU SOLVE A PROBLEM LIKE MARIA? |
| 134 | Do Catholics Honor Mary Too Much? |
| 140 | Explaining Mary, Co-Redemptrix, to an Evangelical |
| 148 | Where is Mary? Images in the Old Testament |
| 151 | Holy Mary, Mother of God |
| 155 | Mother of God or Mother Goddess? |
| 162 | CONCLUSION |
| 162 | All That Catholic Stuff is Connected |

# *Preface*

A nonbeliever recently called in to my radio show with a simple question: "Can you see how some people might regard Catholic claims such as 'God exists,' 'Jesus is the only way to salvation,' and the Catholic Church is the 'one, true Church'?' to be arrogant?"

"Yes." I replied. "I can see how these truth claims could come across as arrogant, at least to someone who doesn't believe them."

I don't think he expected that response and, after a moment of surprised silence, he seemed relieved.

"But what if they're true?" I countered. "What if these statements are actually *true*? Would these truth claims still seem arrogant?"

Would it be "arrogant" for example, to assert that a suspension bridge had the necessary structural strength to support the cars passing over it if the claim were based on sound calculations and fact-based evidence?

No. A skeptic might dispute the claim, but the evidence should persuade him.

Months before the Wright Brothers made their first successful flight on December 17, 1903, several eminent scientists published convincing articles arguing that flight was "impossible."

Though their skeptical arguments seemed plausible, they were proven wrong when the evidence came out. Amazingly, some people still deny that the earth is round, even though evidence disproving their flat-earth theories is overwhelming.

So too, the Catholic Faith and all that it entails—starting with the existence of God, to the resurrection and divinity of Christ and the reality and priority of the Church He established on the rock of Peter is based on evidence. Ample historical, biblical, and rational evidence exists to support and verify claims such as 'God exists,' 'Jesus is the only way to salvation,' and the Catholic Church is the 'one, true Church.'

The problem, however, is that many people nowadays have never encountered this body of convincing evidence. No one has ever presented it to them! Or if they did stumble across it, it wasn't explained in a way they could understand.

This is why Fr. Dwight Longenecker's new book, *An Answer, Not an Argument* is so timely and important for our present generation so shrouded in this present darkness. In these pages Father Longenecker presents a clear, intelligible, ineluctable case for divinity of Jesus Christ, His Resurrection, the Church and the life-changing, grace-filled sacraments He instituted for our salvation. He shows how he entrusted the Virgin Mother to His followers, how a body of doctrines was given to His Apostles to teach to all nations, and how the Holy Spirit inspired the authors to set forth with pen and ink these sacred truths.

As the title of the book emphasizes, everyone deserves not just an argument, but an answer—a *good*, convincing answer to questions about the Faith. Perhaps you'd confess that—if pressed— you might well come up empty handed if someone aimed those arguments at you.

Given his years of experience as a priest, pastor, apologist, and literary guide to all things Catholic, Father Dwight Longenecker is uniquely qualified to guide you, in this book, through an impressive array of Catholic beliefs that many nowadays, often out of ignorance, scoff at and reject as preposterous.

In these pages, he gives reasoned, documented, verifiable answers to the faith-related questions many people have, and he does so in a winsome, low-impact way that offers food for thought to both strengthen the faithful and feed an army of skeptics.

—Patrick Madrid, host of the "Patrick Madrid Show" on Relevant Radio

# *Introduction*

## KNOCKING ON THE DOOR
## OF THE GRAND, OLD MANSION

C. S. Lewis' *Mere Christianity*[1] is one of my favorite books and a classic that has led millions of people to reconsider the Christian faith. It is written in a clear, witty and compelling style that I have tried to use as a standard of my own writing over the years.

At the end of the introduction, Lewis says he is introducing the reader to simple Christianity with no frills or traditions. He writes, "However, I hope no reader will suppose that 'mere' Christianity is here put forward as an alternative to the creeds of the existing communions—as if a man could adopt it in preference to Congregationalism or Greek Orthodoxy or anything else. It is more like a hall out of which doors open into several rooms. If I can bring anyone into the hall, I shall have done what I attempted to do. But it is in the rooms, not in the hall, that there are fires and chairs and meals. The hall is a place to wait in, a place from which to try the various doors, not a place to live in."

In other words, you have to belong to a church if you want to be a Christian. Finding the right church is not always easy, and Lewis says sometimes one has

---

1   C. S. Lewis, *Mere Christianity*, Revised & Enlarged edition (San Francisco: HarperOne, 2015). First published in 1952.

to wait in the hall for some time before finding the right room. He also implies that some people have to visit various rooms before they find the right one. The quest may take a long time, and one may end up waiting during the search.

Then he makes an important point: "When you do get into your room you will find the long wait has done you some kind of good which you would not have had otherwise, but you must regard it as waiting, not as camping. You must keep on praying for light; and of course, even in the hall, you must begin trying to obey the rules which are common to the whole house. And above all, you must be asking which door is the true one, not which pleases you best by its paint and paneling. In plain language, the question should never be: "Do I like that kind of service?" but "Are these doctrines true: Is holiness here? Does my conscience move me towards this? Is my reluctance to knock at this door due to my pride, or my mere taste, or my personal dislike of this particular doorkeeper?"

There is an inconsistency here that even the most fervent of Lewis's admirers must see. Lewis implies that all the rooms off the central hall are of equal value, but he recommends choosing a denomination not according to taste but according to what is true. However, if we must choose according to what is true, then some rooms must be "more true" than others. If this is the case, then the different rooms are not of equal value.

On the other hand, if all the rooms are equally true, then the only criterion for choice is taste and preference, after all. Of course, Lewis is not so relativistic or individualistic as that. He actually says we must choose a church that is true—not a church we like best. If this is the case, then we must keep on searching until we find that church that is "most true." If we find it, according to Lewis, then we must join that church even if we don't necessarily like it.

Notice that this search is for the true church, not the perfect church. In other words, we are looking for a church that holds the truth, not one that has no faults. Many Christians who wish to affirm "mere Christianity" quite rightly conclude that there is no perfect church and they will have to make do with the church they like best. The assumption is that all the side rooms are equally imperfect.

In a sense, this is true, but the equal imperfection of all the churches does not mean they are all equally untrue. Mormons may be more moral than the Methodists, while the Methodists have more truth than the Mormons.

If we are choosing according to perceived perfection or imperfection, we've reduced the whole question once again to personal opinion and we're back to choosing the side room according to which paint and paneling we like best. If Lewis is right that we must choose according to what is most true, then we must look past the human imperfections of any church and try to judge their claim to be most true.

If we are choosing a church that is most true but not necessarily most attractive, then another problem immediately crops up. That is, how do we determine which church is most true? The different churches all seem to have different strengths and weaknesses. Who is to say which is most true? Can we possibly develop some sort of criteria by which to judge? Common sense says a church that is most true will have more truth than the others. In other words, it will be the fullest expression of Christianity. It would make sense therefore to consider questions such as: Which church has thrived and survived in the most places around the world? Which holds the widest expression of different cultures and traditions within it? Which church is both universal and yet identified locally? Which has the largest number of adherents? Which church has stood the test of time? Which has the most impressive historical credentials? Which one has kept the faith despite persecutions from without and problems within? Which church approaches the truth objectively and sticks to it, despite personal cost? Which one exhibits the most impressive holiness? Which one is faithful to Scripture and the historic faith? Which one is intellectually, spiritually, and culturally credible?

To say that a particular church is "more true" is not to judge the goodness or holiness of the individuals in either that church or any other church. The goodness of each person is for God to decide. However, just as some Christians know more about the Bible and the faith than others, so some churches simply have better and more trustworthy credentials. You are more likely to find professional doctors and a full range of treatments in an established modern hospital than at the local health food store. Likewise, you'll find a wider expression of the truth in a large historic church than in an obscure Christian sect.

In looking for the most true church, one will be tempted to look at the outward appearances, but the things that look best on the outside may not be the best when all the facts are gathered. We might see a wrinkled old crone in a shabby cardigan and dismiss her as an alcoholic tramp when in fact she was

Mother Teresa. Likewise, the church that is most true might at first glance seem the least likely candidate. Conversely, the church whose "paint and paneling" we admire may turn out, like a beautiful young woman, to be glamorous but shallow and untrue. It might be that the church that seems most attractive may most likely be the one we should not join. The religion that attracts us might be pandering to the weakest part of our nature.

This collection of essays has been compiled to help non-Catholic Christians examine the questions outlined above. They were written over the years for various different outlets, and this accounts for the variation in tone and accessibility: I wrote for my audience and my audiences varied. I hope the essays will also help Catholic Christians understand their non-Catholic brothers and sisters better. Non-Catholic Christians hold sincere views and usually when they disagree with the Catholic faith, they do so out of sincerely held misunderstandings. They do not disagree with what Catholics believe. They disagree with what they *think* Catholics believe, and those misunderstandings are understandable. They have got their false impressions honestly, not only from their own teachers, but also from the incompetence of many Catholics to explain their beliefs clearly.

So I trust this book will be used by both Catholics and non-Catholics to help all readers to enter into a fuller experience of the Christian faith.

Finally, far be it from me to correct the master, but I think C. S. Lewis' analogy of the hall and side rooms can be expanded. Instead of entering an entrance hall from which one can enter side rooms, I prefer to see the entrance hall as being a lobby of a grand old country mansion. On leaving the waiting room to enter the Catholic faith one does not go into a side room, but an English country house like the one you see on Downton Abbey.

It is a magnificent old house with rooms full of antique furniture, priceless heirlooms, family portraits, a huge gallery lined with armor and weapons, a ballroom, gardens and endless corridors of side rooms where other treasures await. To be sure, the grand old mansion also has an attic full of a dusty jumble of curiosities and artifacts that seem confusing and disturbing. It also has a cellar that is dark and damp and holds secrets that are heartbreaking and terrifying. All of this is part of the Catholic Church, but most of all in that grand old mansion you will find a banqueting hall where the rest of the family meets to await the arrival of the Lord of the Manor who is also the King of Kings.

# *Who Says So?*

## MORE CHRISTIANITY: AFFIRMING NOT DENYING

When I was an Anglican theological student at Oxford, I came across a quotation from the nineteenth century Anglican F. D. Maurice that changed my life. He wrote, "A man is most often right in what he affirms and wrong in what he denies."

It's a quip worth pondering, because if we take it seriously it corrects one of the worst tendencies of human nature in general and religious people in particular. That is the tendency not only to think we are right, but to be convinced that everyone else is wrong. It is the tendency to define our beliefs by what we deny rather than by what we affirm. Protestantism is, by definition, a reaction against something, and that something is the Catholic Church.

At the time of my discovery, I was on a journey from American fundamentalist Christianity to ordination as an Anglican priest. My Protestant background had therefore conditioned me to be skeptical. We were skeptical of non-Christians because they were worldly and unsaved. We were skeptical of Protestants in the mainline denominations because they had "gone liberal." We were skeptical of fellow Evangelicals who were called "Neo-Evangelicals" because they had compromised with the liberals. We were skeptical of most everyone else but ourselves, and most of all we were skeptical of the Catholics.

F. D. Maurice's little dictum made me sit up and think. It was one of those moments of enlightenment, because it was true: In my journey to Anglicanism, whenever I tried to affirm something new, I invariably entered into more truth. Whenever I remained a skeptical and protesting Protestant, I was invariably denying something which had good and positive elements to it.

I resolved at that moment that whenever I came across something new I would try hard to affirm and not deny. I decided to give new ideas, new spiritual practices, new customs and new ways of worship a chance before I rejected them. F. D. Maurice was an old-fashioned liberal, and although I was, by instinct and formation, a conservative, I decided to be liberal in the original sense of the word: that is to say, genuinely open-minded, curious and ready to give the benefit of the doubt.

## *More Christianity*

In time, this approach brought me into the Catholic Church. I had moved from American Evangelical fundamentalism to English Evangelical Anglicanism, and the step from there to Catholicism was the result of my attempt to be open-minded and accepting of ideas and customs that were new and strange to me.

So, for example, when I was invited from the staid and stark worship of Anglican Evangelicalism to experience the Anglo-Catholic worship of Pusey House in Oxford, I went with an open mind. I soon came to understand the statues and candles and incense and vestments. I discovered that I not only understood, but also appreciated, that form of worship. When I encountered a Catholic understanding of the sacraments and the priesthood, I tried to understand and accept, rather than respond with my instinctive Protestant criticism and rejection.

When a friend suggested I visit a Benedictine monastery I drew back in fear and a natural negative bias. "Monks and nuns! They were one of the Catholic Church's big dark secrets!" But I remembered Maurice's thought and gave it a try.

Some years later, a friend came back from a pilgrimage to the great English Marian shrine of Walsingham and brought me a rosary. I can remember holding the beads and feeling repulsed, but then Maurice's quip popped into my mind and I asked myself why a billion Catholics should be wrong and I should be right. I got a book instructing me how to pray the rosary and got started.

After my reception into the Catholic Church, the idea that Catholicism was "more Christianity" (as opposed to C. S. Lewis' *Mere Christianity*) became more and more of a model for my understanding of the faith. Like most converts from another Christian tradition, I never regarded becoming a Catholic as a repudiation of either my homegrown Evangelicalism or my adopted Anglicanism. As a young student, I had explained to my bewildered parents that in becoming an Anglican I was simply adding more things to the wonderful faith they had given me. Becoming a Catholic was to add even more to what I had been given within Anglicanism.

## *But I Agree with You!*

Here are some examples of how the Catholic view adds to the Evangelical view: Catholics, like Evangelicals, believe in the inspiration of the Bible, but while affirming the Evangelical's view of the inspiration of the Bible, the Catholic cannot deny the authority of the Catholic Church. Instead, an Evangelical may want to ask himself why he denies the inspiration of the Church. Doesn't he believe that at Pentecost the Holy Spirit came down and inspired the apostolic Church?

Evangelicals, like Catholics, think Peter was a great missionary, a great warrior for Christ, and a great preacher. Catholics also believe Peter was the leader of the early church, that Jesus gave him a special commission, and that with that commission went special authority. An Evangelical may want to ask himself why, when this is true from the gospels, he denies what is so clear in the Scriptures. Why is he a man of so little faith?

The Evangelical naturally loves Jesus and serves him. He has accepted Jesus Christ as his savior. So have Catholics. We love and serve Jesus Christ. We follow him as our Lord and Savior, but we also honor his Mother Mary.

Evangelicals believe in miracles. So do Catholics. In fact, Catholics believe that a miracle happens every time the priest celebrates Mass. It's a miracle Jesus commanded and said would happen. What a shame that the Evangelical believes in miracles, but limits his belief so much!

Some more examples: Why should Evangelicals deny and reject Jesus' mother? Jesus honored her, the angel Gabriel honored her, Elizabeth honored her, the unborn John the Baptist honored her, Joseph honored her, the shepherds honored her. She said, "All generations shall call me blessed," Catholics have always done so. Why are Evangelicals, who are normally so fervent and loving in their faith, so coldhearted when it comes to the beautiful Mother of Christ?

Why do Evangelicals cling to the Bible alone, while rejecting all other aspects of the historic faith? Prayers to the saints, veneration of icons, liturgy in worship, processions, prayers for the dead, the Mass as a sacrifice, infant Baptism—all these things were also part of the ancient church. Why would Evangelicals keep the Bible, but throw out all the other parts of the early church practice? This is "mere" Christianity indeed! Why so little when he could have so much? Why so small when he could have so largeh? Why such a barren, small and limited understanding of the faith when he could have so much more? And most of all, why would anyone want his religion to be so sterile?

You see how it goes? Evangelicals and Catholics affirm and agree on the good things about their faith. Whenever an Evangelical starts to get negative and start denying Catholic teachings or customs, the Evangelical should ask why he feels that he has to be so negative and so full of denial, protest and rejection. Which sin is worse, believing too much or believing too little? Which is worse, to be guilty of unbelief or to be guilty of being gullible?

When I get to the judgment day I would rather say, "Well, Lord, I'm sorry, I guess I took it all in, hook, line and sinker. Yep, I believed it all: transubstantiation, infallibility of the Pope, the Assumption of the Blessed Virgin, incorrupt saints, stigmata, bleeding statues, I was taken in by the whole lot, and I hope you'll forgive me for being gullible." I'd rather say that than, "I'm sorry, I didn't believe. I was skeptical. I was cynical. I doubted. I spent more time trying to find out what wasn't true, than discovering what was true."

## *Further Up and Further In*

More Christianity gives a firm foundation for apologetics that is not only positive, but expansive in its scope. It keeps the big picture in front of us rather than allowing us to get caught up in the minutiae of argument. Some apologists enjoy the cut and thrust of swapping Biblical texts, quotes from the Fathers of the Church and authoritative statements from theologians and scholars. I prefer to keep to the big picture of affirmation or denial.

This is because, at the end of the day, we are concerned about a person's soul. Most Evangelicals are good Christian souls. They love the Lord with a fervor and keenness that is admirable. They do not wish to be negative or feel that they are narrow in their views or denying the truth that the Lord might have for them. Catholicism at its best is big-hearted and hearty, affirmative and joyful, tolerant and confident, loving and accepting, hrevealing to Evangelicals a perspective on the whole faith which they never knew existed. The good Catholic apologist should be as jolly and wholesome as Chesterton, as bellicose as Belloc and as acute as C. S. Lewis. He should welcome debate as a pathway to truth and a way to go "further up and further in" to God's wonderful truth and life. When this approach works, it makes Catholicism seem full of goodness, truth, beauty, fresh air, humor and an atmosphere that is as big and open as a universal church.

An Answer *Not* An Argument / Fr. Dwight Longenecker

# HOW DO WE KNOW IT'S THE TRUE CHURCH?

My conversion to the Catholic faith began in the world of Protestant fundamentalism. After being brought up in an independent Bible Church, I attended the fundamentalist Bob Jones University. While there, I became an Anglican; later, I went to England to become an Anglican priest.

My pilgrimage of faith came to a crisis in the early 1990s as the Anglican Church struggled over the question of the ordination of women. By instinct, I was against the innovation, but I wanted to be positive and affirm new ideas rather than reject them just because they were new. I decided to put my prejudices to one side and listen as openly as possible to both sides of the debate.

As I listened, I realized that from a human point of view, both the people in favor of women's ordination and those against it had some good arguments. Both sides argued from Scripture, tradition, and reason. Both sides argued from practicality, compassion and justice. Both sides honestly considered their arguments to be persuasive. Furthermore, both sides were composed of prayerful, church-going, sincere Christians who genuinely believed the Holy Spirit was directing them. How could both be right?

From a human point of view, both arguments could be sustained. This led me to a real consideration of the question of authority in the Church. I realized that the divisions over women's ordination in the Anglican Church were no different, in essence, from every other debate that has divided the thousands of Protestant denominations.

In recent years, some groups have split over women's ordination; in other times, others split over whether women should wear hats to church. Going back through the centuries, some groups split over doctrinal issues; others split over moral issues. Whatever the era, whatever the issue and whatever the split, the basic problem is one of authority. If Christians have a sincere disagreement, who decides?

## Wobbly Three-Legged Stool

Evangelical Protestants say the Bible decides, but this begs the question when the two warring parties agree that the Bible is the final authority. They eventually split, because they can't agree about what the Bible actually teaches. I had moved away from the Protestant understanding that Scripture is the only authority, and as an Anglican, believed that authority rested in Scripture, tradition, and reason.

Anglicans call this the "three-legged stool." By turning to Scripture, tradition, and human reason, they hope to have a secure teaching authority. I came to realize, however, that this solution also begs the question. Just as we have to ask the Protestant who believes in *Sola Scriptura*, "Whose interpretation of Scripture?," so we must ask the Anglican, "Whose reason and whose tradition?" In the debate over women's ordination (and now in the debate over homosexuality), both sides appeal to human reason, Scripture and tradition, and they come up with wildly different conclusions.

In the end, the Anglican appeal to a three-legged stool relies just as much on individual interpretation as did the Protestant appeals to *Sola Scriptura*. The three-legged stool turns out to be a theological pogo stick.

## A Son of Benedict Speaks

At about this time, I had a conversation with the Abbot of Quarr Abbey (a Catholic Benedictine monastery on the Isle of Wight). He listened to my situation with compassion and interest. I explained that I did not want to deny women's ordination. I wanted to affirm all things that were good, and I could see some good arguments in favor of women's ordination. He admired this desire to affirm all things, but he said something that set me thinking further:

"Sometimes we have to deny some lesser good in order to affirm the greater good. I think you have to deny women's ordination in order to affirm the apostolic ministry. If the Apostolic authority says no to women's ordination, then to affirm the greater good of apostolic authority, you will have to deny the lesser good of women's ordination. Because if we deny the greater good, then eventually we will lose the lesser good as well."

He hit the nail on the head. His words led me to explore the basis for authority in the Catholic Church. I had read and pretty much accepted the Scriptural support for the Petrine ministry in the Church. I also had come to understand and value the fourfold marks of the True Church—that it is "One, Holy, Catholic and Apostolic." As I studied and pondered the matter further, however, I saw twelve other traits of the church's authority.

## Twelve Traits of Authority

These twelve traits—in six paired sets—helped me to understand how comprehensive and complete the Catholic claims of authority are. I came to realize that other churches and ecclesial bodies might claim some of the traits, but only the Catholic Church demonstrates all twelve fully.

What are the twelve traits of authority, and how do they work? We have to ask what a group of Christians who were deliberating a difficult matter would need to make their decision.

### It Is Rooted in History . . .

First of all, it seems clear that their decision would have to be made from a historical perspective. It would not be good enough to decide complex moral, social, or doctrinal issues based on popularity polls or yesterday's newspaper. To decide difficult questions, a valid authority has to be historical.

By this, I mean not only must it have an understanding of history, but it must be rooted in history itself. In addition, the authority has to show a real continuity with the historical experience of Christianity. The churches that have existed for four or five hundred years can demonstrate this to a degree, but only the Catholic (and Eastern Orthodox) Church has a living link with history that goes back to Roman times—and then, through Judaism, back to the beginning of human history.

### . . . and Adaptable

The historical link is essential, but on its own it is not sufficient. Historical authority has to be balanced with the ability to be up to date. An authority that is only historical becomes ossified. It never changes. An authority that cannot be up to date is not just rooted in history, it is bound by history. A valid authority structure needs to be flexible and adaptable. Christians face complex modern moral and doctrinal dilemmas. A valid authority system draws on the wisdom of the past to rule properly on the questions of the present.

## *It Is Objective . . .*

A third quality of a valid authority system is that it needs to be objective. By this, I mean it needs to be independent of any one person's or group's agenda, ideology, philosophy or self-interest. A valid authority transcends all political, economic, and cultural pressures. The objective quality of this authority system also allows it to make decisions that are unpopular or that go against the spirit of the times and majority opinion.

An objective authority is based on certain universal basic assumptions, immutable principles, and observable and undeniable premises. From these objective criteria, the valid authority system builds its teaching.

## *. . . and Flexible*

For the authority to be valid, however, it cannot rely on abstract principles and objective criteria alone. The valid authority is suitably subjective in applying objective principles. In other words, it understands the complexities of real life and the pastoral exigencies of helping real people. As a result, the valid authority can apply its objective principles in a flexible, practical, and down-to-earth manner. The Catholic authority system does just that. Throughout the Code of Canon Law, for example, we are reminded that the law is there to serve the people of God in their quest for salvation.

Individual Christians, or particular Christian groups, often fall into one side of this pair or the other. The rigorists or legalists want everything to be objective and "black and white" all the time, while the liberals or sentimentalists want every decision to be relative, open-ended, and flexible according to the pastoral needs. Only the Catholic system can hold the two in tension, because only the Catholic system has an infallible authority which can keep the two sides balanced.

## *It Is Universal . . .*

An authority that can speak to all situations can only do so if it comes from a universal source. This source of authority needs to be universal not only geographically, but also chronologically. In other words, it transcends national agendas and limitations, but it also transcends the cultural trends and intellectual fashions of any particular time. Every church or ecclesial structure other than the Catholic Church is limited, either by its historical foundations or by its cultural and national identity.

For example, the Eastern Orthodox find it very hard to transcend their national identity, while the churches of the Reformed tradition struggle to transcend the particular cultural issues that surrounded their foundation. The national, cultural, and chronological identities of other ecclesial bodies limit their ability to speak with a universal voice. When they do move away from their foundations, they usually find themselves at sea amidst the fashions and trends of the present day. They also find that they lose their distinctive identities when they drift from their foundations. A universal authority system, on the other hand, transcends both chronological and geographical limitations.

## . . and Local

However, this universal authority needs to be applied in a particular and local way. An authority that is only universal remains vague, abstract, and disincarnate, that is, without any physical grounding. For a universal authority system to be valid, it also must be expressed locally. Catholicism speaks with a universal voice, but it is also as local as St. Patrick's Church and Fr. Magee on the corner of Chestnut Street.

Not only does the universal Church have a local outlet, but that outlet has a certain autonomy which allows it to be flexible in its application of the universal authority. Catholicism travels well, and because of the universal authority structure, it can allow far more varieties of enculturation at the local level than churches which are more bound by the time and place of their foundations.

## It Is Intellectually Challenging . . .

The fourth pair of characteristics that demonstrate the validity of the Catholic authority system include its intellectual satisfaction and its accessibility. If an authority system is to speak to the complexities of the human situation, then it must be able to hold its own with the philosophical and intellectual experts in every field of human endeavor. What other ecclesial system can marshal experts from every area of human expertise to speak authoritatively in matters of faith and morals? Time and again, the Catholic Church has been able to speak with authority about the spiritual dimension of economics, ethics, politics, diplomacy, the arts, and philosophy.

This authority must not only be able to hold its own with the intellectual experts in all fields, but it must be intellectually satisfying and coherent within itself. A unified and complete intellectual system must be able to explain the world as it is. Furthermore, this intellectual system must continually develop and be re-expressed—always interpreting ageless truth in a way that is accessible for the age in which it lives. This intellectual system must be an integral and vital part of the religion, while also being large enough to self-criticize. Only the Catholic faith has such an all-encompassing, impressive system of teaching.

### . . . and Accessible to the Uneducated

Nonetheless, while the authority system must be intellectually top-notch, the religious system must also be accessible to peasants and the illiterate. A religious system that is only intellectual or appeals merely to the literate can speak only for the intellectuals and literate.

Some denominations appeal to the simple and unlearned, but have trouble keeping the top minds. Others appeal to the educated elite, but lose the masses. Catholicism, on the other hand, is a religion of the greatest minds of history and the religion of the ignorant. It is a religion that is complex enough for St. Thomas Aquinas and simple enough for St. Joseph of Cupertino. It has room at the manger for both the Magi and the shepherds.

### It Is Visible . . .

As a Protestant, I was taught that the Church was invisible. That is, it consisted of all people everywhere who believed in Jesus, and that the true members of the Church were known to God alone. This is true, but there is more to it than that. Invisibility and visibility make up the fifth paired set of characteristics that mark the truly authoritative church.

The Church is made up of all people everywhere who trust in Christ. However, this characteristic alone is not satisfactory, because human beings locked in the visible plane of reality also demand that the Church be visible.

Even those who believe only in the invisible church belong to a particular church which they attend every Sunday. Those who believe only in the invisible church must logically conclude that it doesn't really matter which church they go to.

### ... and Invisible

The Catholic system of authority recognizes both the invisible dimension of the Church and the visible. The Church is greater than what we can observe, but the church we observe is also greater than we think. The invisible Church subsists in the Catholic Church, and while you may not be able to identify the extent of the invisible Church, you can with certainty point to the Catholic Church and say, "There is the Body of Christ."

A few small Protestant denominations claim that their visible church is the true church, but their claims have no foundation, because they have none of the other twelve traits of true authority. Because it has all these traits, only the Catholic Church can claim to be the living, historical embodiment of the Body of Christ on earth.

### It is Both Human and Divine

Finally, for the church to speak with authority it must be both human and divine. An authority that speaks only with a divine voice lacks the authenticity that comes with human experience. So Islam and Mormonism, which are both based on a book supposedly dictated by angels, are unsatisfactory because their authority is supernaturally imposed on the human condition.

On the other hand, a religion that is purely a construct of the human condition is merely a system of good works, religious techniques, or good ideas. Christian Science or Unitarianism, for example, were developed only from human understandings and natural goodness. As such, both lack a supernatural voice of authority.

The Judeo-Christian story, however, is both human and divine. The voice of authority is always expressed through human experience and human history. Divine inspiration in the Judeo-Christian tradition is God's word spoken through human words. This incarnated form of authority finds its fulfillment in Jesus Christ, who hands on his totally incarnated authority to Peter and his successors.

## *Built upon the Rock*

Some churches may exercise some of the twelve traits, but only the Catholic Church is able to field all twelve as a foundation for decision-making. When the Catholic Church pronounces on any difficult question, the response is historical, but up to date. It is based on objective general principles, but it applies to specific needs. The Church's authority transcends space and time, but it is relevant to a particular place and time. Its truths will be intellectually profound, but expressed in a way that is simple enough for anyone to apply. Finally, it will express truths that are embedded in the human experience, but spring from divine inspiration.

This authority works infallibly through the active ministry of the whole Church. The *Catechism of the Catholic Church* says that it is Christ who is infallible, and he grants a measure of his infallibility to his body, the Church. That infallibility is worked out through these twelve traits, but it is expressed most majestically and fully through Christ's minister of infallibility: one person—the Rock on which the Church is built, Peter and his successors.

# WHAT IS TRUTH?

## *An Examination of Sola Scriptura*

Pontius Pilate asked the basic question for all humanity when he asked Jesus, "What is Truth?" The irony of the scene is powerful and poignant because the Eternal Truth stood before him incarnate as a human person. In John 14:16 Jesus had said, "I am the Way, the Truth and the Life." Later in the gospel Peter said, "Where else shall we go Lord, but to you? You alone have the words of eternal life" (John 6:68). So the Christian answer is that Jesus himself is the Truth. If you want the Truth, come to him.

That's something all Christians agree on, but that answer raises more questions. The next question is—how do we come to know Jesus as truth? How do we get in touch with this Jesus who is truth? We need answers to specific questions—what should we believe? How shall we behave? How shall we run the church? Jesus may be the Truth, but how do we get hold of that truth? How do we know that what we believe is his truth?

In my evangelical days, I was told the truth was to be found in the Bible and in the Bible alone. In my Bible lessons at Bob Jones I memorized a famous and important verse—2 Timothy 3:16–17:

> All Scripture is given by inspiration of God and is useful for doctrine, for instruction, for correction and training in righteousness so the man of God man be fully equipped for every good work.

In other words—the Bible was where we turned to learn what to believe and how to behave. And we believed the Bible because it is inspired—it is God-breathed.

But there are some problems with this view. A simple problem is that since 2 Timothy 3:16–17 is in the New Testament, it can't refer to the New Testament. Paul—in writing to Timothy—is only talking about the Old Testament Scriptures.

But let's say for the sake of argument that it does refer to the New Testament too. While the verse certainly says the Scripture is inspired and that it should be used to determine doctrine and Christian behavior—it doesn't say that Scripture is the *only* authority for God's truth. And in fact nowhere in the Bible do you find such a thing stated. In addition—if this is the only evidence for Biblical inspiration, a problem arises as soon as you start to push things a little.

The problem is this: 2 Timothy 3:16 says, "All Scripture is given by inspiration of God," and this is used to prove that Scripture is inspired. But how do we know that 2 Timothy 3:16 is itself inspired? The reasoning is circular. It goes like this:

We believe the Bible. OK—why is that? Because it is inspired. Why do we believe it is inspired? Because the Bible says it is inspired and we believe the Bible. OK, how do we know the Bible is inspired? Because the Bible says it is inspired and we believe the Bible because it is inspired. Too much of this type of reasoning makes you dizzy. There has to be a better answer.

If that was one problem, I also had another difficulty by the time I got to Bible college. I had always been taught that the Bible was simple to understand, and the simple gospel message was straightforward. But this caused a problem. If the gospel message was simple and straightforward, why were there so many different Christian denominations all in disagreement with each other?

When I asked a teacher, I was told that the different denominations agreed on the basics—which were plain and easily understood from Scripture, but they disagreed on the extras. But when I examined what the different denominations taught, they not only disagreed on little things like whether women should wear hats to church or whether you had to be baptized by immersion or sprinkling, but they also disagreed on important things like Baptism, communion, how you should be saved, who was in charge of the church, who was going to heaven and many other things. If Scripture was the only source of authority, shouldn't the Church be united around one simple, clear teaching from Scripture?

Another verse I had to memorize was 2 Peter 1:20: "No scripture is of any private interpretation, but holy men of God spake as the Holy Spirit instructed them." Obviously, all the different Christian denominations disagreed. They all had different interpretations of the Bible, and they were all convinced that their interpretation was right. And if they all had different interpretations of the Bible, then they must be interpreting them on their own—but 2 Peter 1:20 says that the Bible cannot be interpreted privately. Something was wrong here.

So I wound up with two basic problems:

If the Bible gave the only support for its own inspiration, then it was proving itself and that didn't seem to work. There had to be some other authority which could validate the inspiration of the Bible.

If the Bible was the only source of authority for Christians, then why were all the different churches so divided? There had to be some other authority which could decide how the Bible was to be understood.

In the face of these questions, a lot of people nowadays give up believing in the inspiration of the Bible. About the disagreements in the Church they say, "Well, you can't really know the right interpretation—we have to live with these disagreements."

But can that be true? Is it possible that Jesus called himself the Way, the Truth and the Life and commanded his apostles to go out into all the world to preach the gospel if, at the end of the day, we can't really know what is true after all? Is it possible that we have a gospel to proclaim, but God hasn't provided a certain way for us to know what that gospel consists of and how it is applied? We've ended up like Pontius Pilate—shrugging our shoulders and saying cynically—"Ahh—What is 'truth' anyway?"

In fact, there are some excellent rock-solid answers for these questions. The Bible *is* inspired, but the evidence for its inspiration rests on something more than 2 Timothy 3:16. There is also a sure-fire way to know the right interpretation of the Bible, but the evidence for that sure interpretation is profound and goes to the very roots of Scripture itself.

The Bible didn't just drop down out of heaven. Although we believe it was inspired by God, this inspiration happened through real people in real situations in real places and times. The Scriptures were written by the people of God, for the people of God. They were read by the people of God, used to teach the people of God, and used for the worship of the people of God. Maybe the best way to describe the Bible is to say that it is the "story of the people of God"—the Church—both the Old Testament Church and the New Testament Church. The Bible was never just a list of things about God which His people must believe. Neither was it a set of rules to be obeyed. Instead, the Bible was first and foremost the story of God's loving relationship with humanity.

Furthermore, the same people who wrote the Scriptures—used the Scriptures, prayed the Scriptures and learned from the Scriptures—chose which holy writings should be included as Scripture. By the end of the first century after Christ, the Jews made a final decision about which of their writings were to make up the scriptures that we call the Old Testament. By A.D. 130, the early Christians were unanimous in accepting the four gospels and the thirteen letters of Paul. By 170, the church leaders had put these writings on the same level as the Old Testament, and within another two hundred years—by the year 369—we have the first list of the same New Testament books which we all agree on. Then in 382 at the Council of Rome, the whole church agreed on a list of all the Old and New Testament books.

History shows that from the beginning there has been an extraordinary group of people who claimed to be God's chosen people. The Christian church was founded by a clear and direct act of God's inspiration at Pentecost. Just as the Old Testament people of God were guided by a pillar of fire—representing the Holy Spirit—so the New Testament Church is a holy people—guided by the Holy Spirit of Pentecost. This community of faith is a fact of history. That it is guided and protected by God is also historically evident. Because it speaks with Spirit-filled authority the Church—the people of God who were inspired to write the Scriptures—can also validate the inspiration of the Bible.

So Catholics say the Bible is inspired NOT just because 2 Timothy 3:16 says so, but also because the Bible is the product of the people of God. The Bible is inspired because it is the product of the Spirit-filled Church. The inspired people of God wrote the Scriptures, used the Scriptures, prayed the Scriptures and chose which writings were to be considered Scripture, and that is why we believe the Bible to be inspired.

## *The Authority of the Church*

The truth in the Bible comes to us through the experience of the Church. This matches up exactly with Paul's view. In 1 Timothy 3:15 he says something very important: "God's church is the household of the living God, the pillar and foundation of truth," and in Ephesians 3:10 he says that it is God's "intent that through the church the manifold wisdom of God should be made known."

In other words, it is through the Church that we learn the truth about Jesus—not just the Bible. It is by belonging to the living body of Christ—the Church—that we come to understand and know the mystery of Jesus Christ himself.

Paul says the Church is the pillar and foundation of truth. So the Church is the basis for the truth, the support for the truth—it is on the Church that the whole edifice rests and is supported. Without the Church, the whole thing is built on sand. Not only does the Church establish and validate the inspiration of the Bible, and not only was the Bible the product of the Church's life, but the Church also determined which books went into the Bible. It's no exaggeration to say that without the Church we wouldn't have a Bible at all.

As a result, Catholics conclude that even today you cannot have the Scriptures without the Church. The two pillars of Scripture and the Church's teaching stand together. The Scriptures offer the inspired Word of God and the Church's Teaching offers the God-given interpretation of the Word. Catholics believe that the Bible is interpreted by a living, dynamic, spirit-filled Church, and that from Pentecost onward this Church has always passed its teaching on from one generation to the next in both written forms.

But the church did not only pass the teaching on in written form. From the earliest days, the teaching was also passed on through an oral tradition. By "tradition," Catholics don't mean dead religious customs, ceremonies, rules and regulations. Instead, when Catholics speak of "tradition," we are referring to a body of teaching which is formed by the experience of the Church. A body of teaching which is at once ancient and yet fresh and alive.

Is this what the early Church believed? Did Paul rest his faith only in the Scriptures? He certainly rested them in the Old Testament Scriptures. He told Timothy, "devote yourself to the public reading of Scripture, to preaching and to teaching." Elsewhere he told Timothy to "continue in what you have learned . . . because you know those from whom you learned it and how from infancy you have known the holy Scriptures" (2 Tim. 3:14–15).

Paul believed in the Old Testament. He also believed that his own writings were to be taken as authoritative for determining doctrine and right Christian behavior. But he also believed his other teachings were authoritative as well. That strand of apostolic teaching wasn't written down. It is the inspired preaching of the apostles, and this oral teaching and preaching comes directly from God, as does the written word.

Jesus said to his apostles in Luke 10:16 that "whoever listens to you listens to me." In 2 Peter 3:2, Peter pointed out that the word of the apostles comes as from the Lord himself and in Galatians 1:11–12 Paul proclaimed, "I want you to know that the gospel I preached is not something that man made up. I did not receive it from any man, nor was I taught it; rather I received it by revelation from Jesus Christ." Peter in 1 Peter 1:24–25 called this divinely inspired preaching the "living and enduring word of God." and said that it would stand for ever. So along with the written word of God there was to be an enduring oral tradition—a teaching which would be passed on from generation to generation.

Paul stated this most clearly in 2 Thessalonians 2:15. There he said, "So then brothers, stand firm and hold to the traditions we passed on to you whether by word of mouth or by letter." So the teachings which Paul received from Jesus he passed on both in writing and by word of mouth.

Some people say that the word of mouth tradition ceased once the Bible books were written, but Paul acknowledges that both sources of teaching existed when he wrote to the Thessalonians. We also see that Paul not only received this oral tradition from others, but he also passed it on to his hearers. In 1 Corinthians 15:2–3 he said, "By this gospel you are saved if you hold firmly to the word I preached to you. . . . For what I received I passed on to you as of the first importance."

Paul knows the importance of the oral teaching as well as the written teaching because he tells Timothy in 2 Timothy 1:13 to faithfully guard the oral teaching which he had received. So he writes, "What you heard from me keep as the pattern of sound teaching with faith and love in Jesus Christ guard the good deposit which is entrusted to you." Elsewhere he praises the Corinthians for "upholding the traditions which I have passed on to you" (1 Cor. 11:2).

Catholics believe that this ancient teaching of the apostles has been handed on from generation to generation and kept alive by the constant and continual life of the Church—the new people of God. Did Paul think this oral teaching was to be passed on? Paul said to Timothy in 2 Timothy 2:2: "And the things you have heard me say in the presence of many witnesses entrust to reliable men who will also be qualified to teach others." In other words, he commanded Timothy to hand on the oral tradition which he had received from Paul.

## *The Deposit of Faith in the Early Church Fathers*

The documents of the early Church in the years just after the death of the apostles show that they believed their Church leaders had inherited a precious deposit of faith—both in the writings of the apostles and in the oral traditions of the apostles. In about A.D. 95 a Church leader in Rome called Clement wrote to the church at Corinth that "the apostles received the gospel for us from the Lord Jesus Christ."[1] He goes on to explain how that gospel has been faithfully handed down to his church from one generation to another.

Writing about the year 189, Irenaeus, a bishop in the French city of Lyon, wrote: "What if the apostles had not left writings to us? Would it not be necessary to follow the order of tradition which was handed down to those to whom they entrusted the churches?"[2] Elsewhere Irenaeus also pointed out how important this apostolic tradition is for people to know the full truth. "It is possible then for everyone in every church who may wish to know the truth to contemplate the Traditions of the Apostles which has been made known throughout the whole world."[3]

This helps us answer the difficult question—where do we turn for a faithful interpretation of the Bible? Is there a body of teaching which has been faithfully passed down from the apostles that would help us to interpret the Scriptures the right way? If such a body of teaching exists, then it provides a rich mine for us to turn to when we try to interpret the Scripture. If an ancient strand of teaching exists which goes back to the apostles themselves, then we have not only the Scripture for a source book, but we have a rich tapestry of teaching which helps us to understand the Scripture.

As Catholics, we believe that we have just such a source for properly interpreting the Bible. When we have a difficult question of Biblical interpretation, we don't just read the rest of the Bible to find the answer to

---

1   *1 Clement*, 42.

2   Irenaeus of Lyons, *Against Heresies*, 4.1.

3   Irenaeus of Lyons, *Against Heresies*, 3.1.

the difficult question. We turn to the tradition to see what the people of God believed before us. Did they face the same question? How did they answer it? Did they face a similar circumstance? How did they confront it? Did they face the same doubts, problems, heresies and attacks? How did they stand up for the truth in their day? How can it help us determine the truth today?

## *The Guidance of the Holy Spirit*

From the beginning, the gospel of salvation was passed on by both word of mouth and by a living oral tradition of teaching. Eventually the written Word came to be collected together into what we know as the New Testament, but that didn't mean that the dynamic, infilling Holy Spirit ceased to function in the Church. We know that the Spirit of Pentecost is still poured out on the Church—guiding and protecting and teaching. In John 16:13 Jesus promised that the Holy Spirit—who guides the Church—would lead his apostles into all truth, and in John 14:16 Jesus promises that the Holy Spirit would be with the apostles forever.

Second Peter states: "No prophecy of Scripture is of any private interpretation" (2 Pet. 1:20). So if we are not to interpret the Scripture on our own, who is to interpret it for us? Jesus said the Holy Spirit will guide us into all truth, so the Holy Spirit plays a part. But Peter himself answers the question in the same epistle. In verses 16–18 of chapter one of the same epistle, Peter claimed teaching authority because he was an eyewitness of Jesus' life and glory and got the truth direct from Jesus. He then said in verse 2 of chapter 3 that the truth was spoken in the past by the holy prophets and the commands are now given by Jesus Christ through the apostles.

What is important to see here is that Peter compares the role of the New Testament apostles to the Old Testament prophets. The prophets were directly inspired by God. Their preaching was considered to be a direct word from God to the people of God. We have already seen that Peter considered his preaching to be "the Word of God which stands forever." As such, the apostles are the prophets—the God-inspired teachers of the New Testament people of God. When Peter says "No prophecy of Scripture is of any private interpretation" he also means that only the prophet, that is, the apostle, is entitled and empowered by the Holy spirit to give the right interpretation.

Paul agrees with him. In Ephesians 3:5, he says the mystery of God has now been revealed by the Spirit to God's holy apostles and prophets. And it is the same Spirit-led group of men who are the foundation of the church—so Paul says in chapter 2 verse 20 that the Ephesians are members of the Church— the household of God which is built on the foundation of the apostles and prophets with Christ Jesus as the chief corner stone. Jesus is the corner stone of this Church, but it is the apostles and the prophets—inspired by God's Holy Spirit—who provide the foundation for the Church (Cf. Rev. 21:14).

This verse fits together with Paul's other teaching that the Church is the "pillar and foundation of truth" (1Tim. 3:15). So the Church—based on the teaching of the apostles—is the source for Scripture, and who can rightly interpret the Scripture? The same apostolic Church continues to be the faithful interpreter of the Scripture. The Church which was inspired to write the Scripture and inspired to choose which books went into the Bible is also the chosen, Spirit-filled interpreter of Scripture.

## *Where does one find this apostolic Church today?*

If it's true that the apostles were the ones to interpret Scripture, and the apostolic Church was therefore the one to interpret Scripture, does that same apostolic authority exist today? Does the apostolic Church exist today? If so, where can we find it? We have seen that Paul explicitly handed on his teaching authority to Timothy and commanded him to hand on that authority to others who would in turn hand it on to their successors.

Timothy wasn't the only one. Paul also sent Titus to Crete to organize the Church there. He calls Titus his son in the faith and says, "The reason I left you behind in Crete was for you to get everything organized there and to appoint elders in every town the way I told you" (Titus 1:5). And what kind of a man must this elder be? "He must have a firm grasp of the word as taught so that he can be counted on to expound sound doctrine" (Titus 1:9). So in the New Testament we see Paul clearly setting up the Church with his sons in the faith as his successors in the various locations.

The writings of the early Church testify that the first generation of Christians after the apostles believed their Church leaders had somehow inherited the same teaching authority that the apostles had.

So Clement—the leader of the Roman Church around A.D. 95—writes:

> The Apostles received the gospel for us from the Lord Jesus Christ . . . and they went out full of confidence in the Holy Spirit . . . and appointed their first fruits . . . to be bishops and deacons. Our apostles knew there would be strife on the question of the bishop's office. Therefore, they appointed these people already mentioned and later made further provision that if they should fall asleep other tested men should succeed to their ministry.[4]

So Clement of Rome believed the apostles—one of whom may still have been alive—had wished for their teaching office to be continued in the Church.

Ignatius of Antioch was martyred in the year 115. In writing to the Trallian Church, he equates the Church elders with apostles: "Submit yourselves also to the priests as to the Apostles of Jesus Christ."[5]

And Irenaeus, who wrote around A.D. 180, also believed firmly that the Church had inherited the authority of the apostles to teach the truth faithfully. According to him, it is because the Church leaders have inherited the apostolic authority that they can interpret Scripture properly. So he writes,

> By knowledge of the truth we mean: the teaching of the Apostles; the order of the Church as established from earliest times throughout the world . . . preserved through the episcopal succession: for to the bishops the apostles committed the care of the church in each place which has come down to our own time safeguarded by . . . the most complete exposition . . . the reading of the Scriptures without falsification and careful and consistent exposition of them avoiding both rashness and blasphemy.

Remembering that Paul handed on his teaching authority to Timothy and Titus, and seeing how through history that authority has been handed down from generation to generation, Catholics believe that the dynamic and living teaching authority continues to live within the Catholic bishops. It is they who have received their ministry in direct line from the apostles, passed down over the last 2,000 years.

---

[4] *1 Clement*, 42–44.

[5] Ignatius of Antioch, *Epistle to the Trallians*, 2.

Because of this direct link, Catholics believe the Church has a living connection with the apostolic authority, and that within the living apostolic tradition of the Catholic Church we can find a rock-solid, sure, historic and unified body of teaching which illuminates and interprets the Bible without fail.

# BEING ONE, HOLY, CATHOLIC AND APOSTOLIC

## *How to Be One*

Every Sunday in the Nicene Creed, Catholics and many Protestants affirm that we believe in "One, Holy, Catholic and Apostolic Church." What does this mean in real life? Too often, we treat the creed like one of those terms of agreement you have to click on before they will let you on to a website. We rattle through the creed dutifully, not giving it too much thought.

The creed is not just an intellectual formulation of our faith. Every word in the creed has a practical application to our lives. The creed is not simply a centuries-old list of dogmas we affirm with a nod of the head. The creed doesn't just tell us what to think, it tells us how to think and therefore how to live. The creed is not a dead document, but a springboard to a more vibrant spiritual life.

Our society is riddled through with false philosophies that contradict our Catholic faith. The creed gives us clarity. It helps us analyze these false ways of thinking. The false philosophies are not something we adopt consciously. Instead, they are a set of assumptions that lie at the root of our secular society, and then filter through every aspect of our lives. We are influenced by these false beliefs constantly, through advertising and through all the media messages we receive from the multitude of secular sources, every moment of our waking lives.

Through four sections I'll be exploring the four marks of the Church we affirm in the creed, along with twelve different "isms"—twelve false foundational philosophies that are woven into our popular culture. These twelve false philosophies infect many of our decisions as Catholics. We've sucked up the secular culture without even knowing it, and we think things through from a worldly point of view. We make decisions and take actions based not on a deeply Catholic way of thinking, but on a secular mindset.

The twelve "isms" are gathered into four groups of three, and these twelve false philosophies are countered by the four marks of the Church: One, Holy, Catholic and Apostolic.

The first of the false philosophies which underlies our society is Syncretism. A person is syncretistic when he gathers his beliefs from a range of different sources. The syncretist follows a pick 'n' mix philosophy. His belief system is a hotch potch in a hot pot. It's a melting pot of information picked up from the web, along with insights from one's education, a smidgen of religion here, some pop psychology, stuff picked up in travels, popular ideas from TV and new media. The syncretist rejects any unified and integrated belief system—picking up ideas and abandoning them as they seem attractive at the time.

Syncretism is linked with the second "ism"—Individualism. Individualism exalts the individual over any authority, structure, institution, or belief system. The individualist is the sole arbiter of what is beautiful, true and good. The assumption undergirding individualism is that every person's judgement is just as valid as the next person's. No one, therefore, has a right to tell anyone else what to do. Because there is not greater authority to decide what is wrong, no one must judge another. Judging others is perceived as intolerance, and for the individualist this is the worst sin.

Think of these three "isms" as three sisters. Sister Syncretism is a fat and lazy girl who simply takes on whatever belief system seems attractive at the time. Sister Individualism is a strident campaigner for her own rights and her own independence against all authority structures. The third sister is a sweet and attractive girl. She is called Sister Sentimentalism.

Sister Sentimentalist decides everything according to her emotions. She wants everything to be nice, and wants everyone to feel good. She doesn't want anything nasty to happen. The sentimentalist is "saddened" when things are harsh and intolerant. With such a longing for happiness and light, the sentimentalist seems the sweetest of the sisters. However, when things don't go her way (especially when someone makes an objective judgement) Sister Sentimentalist can become strident like her sister the individualist.

These three secular "isms" are determined by one shared attribute: all three elevate individual judgement over all authority. Therefore, the three ugly sisters are countered by knowing and living the truth that the Catholic Church is "One."

Syncretism is replaced by a unified teaching authority that draws all truth together, sifts through it, discerns error, teaches truth, and organizes it all in one integrated belief system. The unified teaching authority of the church draws each individual into a harmonious grouping—valuing each individual as an eternal soul, but also calling each individual into one, integrated Body of Christ in the Church. Being "One" in the church also subordinates sentimentalism. Our emotions and feelings are important, but they are secondary motives for our actions and beliefs. Unity or "being One" brings our strong but unreliable emotions into their proper relationship to the unified truth.

How do we turn away from Syncretism, Individualism and Sentimentalism to be "One"? We do so through our daily submission to the unified authority of the Church. We are encouraged to study and understand other belief systems and draw good things from them, but we do this while constantly learning more about our own unified faith.

Being One means that our individual lives and emotions are harnessed to a greater, unified cause. To be One, we are constantly subjecting our own individual beliefs, desires and goals to the greater unity of the Catholic Church.

Critics might say that this turns us into religious zombies—simply going along in mindless obedience to the will of our overlords. Not so. It is within true unity that we link our own individual lives to something far greater and older and better, and through this transaction our lives open out and we participate in God's greater plan for the world.

What are the practical ways to become "One"? Praying the Divine Office unifies us with all other Catholics who are praying with us each day. Most of all we become "One" as we worship together at Mass. Mass is the place where we are unified in the mystical Body of Christ. It is there that we see the church being One, Holy, Catholic and Apostolic, and it is there that we join our lives in that same unity.

## *How to Be Holy*

When we recite the creed each Sunday and say, "I believe in One, Holy, Catholic and Apostolic Church" most of us don't imagine that it has much to do with our everyday lives. Stop! Every aspect of our faith has a practical application. Faith works. Our beliefs are held for good reasons. If we practice them, our life changes for the better. If we neglect them, our life dwindles into chaos and emptiness. The creed teaches us not only what to think, but how to think.

The words "One, Holy, Catholic and Apostolic" connect with foundational philosophies in our lives. In this chapter, we are exploring twelve different "isms" that lie at the foundation of our country's secular worldview. These false philosophies are embedded deeply in our assumptions. They infect our worldview whether we like it or not. Our Catholic faith can be polluted by anti-Catholic belief systems right at the source. These anti-Catholic belief systems are just "there." They undergird the advertising we look at, the music we listen to, the movies we watch, the books we read and the education we receive.

In the previous section, I exposed three "isms" that work against unity: Syncretism, Individualism and Sentimentalism. The first of the next set of three is Scientism. In his encyclical *Fides et Ratio*, Pope St. John Paul II defines Scientism as,

> the philosophical notion which refuses to admit the validity of forms of knowledge other than those of the positive sciences; and it relegates religious, theological, ethical and aesthetic knowledge to the realm of mere fantasy.[1]

The follower of Scientism assumes that the only valid form of knowledge is that which is tested by the scientific method. Remember, to be against Scientism is not to be against science. The problem is not science, but Scientism—the belief that only scientifically verified knowledge is worthwhile. This philosophy is very widespread. Throughout our educational systems and in the media and academia, it is assumed that modern science and technology have "disproved" religion.

These three false "isms" are also like three ugly sisters, and the second sister is Utilitarianism. This is the belief that if something does the job, that is all that matters. The bottom line is efficiency and economy. It is a good thing for our machinery to work efficiently, and we all want the best solution at the lowest price. However, to judge a thing only by its usefulness or price is a form of brutality. When we follow Utilitarianism, we end up knowing the price of everything and the value of nothing.

Utilitarianism seems cheerfully practical. It seems right, but the completely practical and cost-effective person ends up being cruel. People are treated like machines. Either they do the job or they don't. If they don't, they are out. Unnecessary employees are "terminated." Even worse, human lives are judged according to their practicality or cost. Does it seem too expensive

---

1   John Paul II, *Fides et Ratio*, 88.

to have a baby? The utilitarian says, "Abort the pregnancy." Is it too expensive to keep old people, who have outlived their usefulness alive? The utilitarian solution is to put them to sleep.

If these three "isms" are sisters, then Scientism is a blue stocking—an academic snob and Sister Utilitarian is a brisk, no-nonsense, Nurse Ratchet. The third sister is Mother Materialism. By "Materialism," I don't mean "shop until you drop." A better word for that type of greed or acquisitiveness is "consumerism." Instead, Materialism is a deeper philosophy which holds that the material world is all there is. Beneath both Utilitarianism and Scientism is the assumption that there is no supernatural realm. What you see is what you get. Mother Materialism is a cynical old woman who sees through everything.

The materialist can also be an atheist, for if the physical realm is all there is, then there is no God, no judgement, no hope of heaven, and no risk of hell. With such a philosophy, a man can do anything he wants. Thus, Materialism and her sisters Scientism and Utilitarianism turn out to be not just three ugly sisters, but three monstrous gorgons who will (in the name of usefulness and the right price) terminate the weak, the vulnerable or anyone who stands in their way.

It is easy to believe that we Catholics wouldn't live by such terrible set of beliefs, but we make choices according to usefulness and the right price all the time, and often we make choices that go against higher principles just to get a bargain or make our lives more efficient or easy. Furthermore, don't we often regard the Church in practical terms? We think the church is to "make the world a better place" or to make our lives better.

The antidote to Materialism, Scientism and Utilitarianism is the second mark of the Church. By being "One," we counter Individualism, Sentimentalism and Syncretism. By being "Holy," we counter Utilitarianism, Scientism and Materialism. In this instance, I am using the word "Holy" to indicate our belief in the supernatural. Holiness is only accomplished through the infusion of God's supernatural grace in our lives, and the only way to counter the brutal beliefs of Utilitarianism, Materialism and Scientism is to fully affirm the existence of the supernatural realm, and its daily interaction with our world.

Being "Holy" in this sense does not just mean being pious. It means learning to see the supernatural dimension behind the natural realm. It means having eyes to see the hand of God at work in and through and beneath and beyond all we can see. We develop this way of being "Holy" by increasing spiritual awareness in all that we do, but especially in our worship.

If we prayed and practiced our faith with a trembling awareness of the supernatural dimension, the temptation to value things only according to their usefulness or price would disappear. If we prayed and went to Mass more reverently—truly believing in the supernatural dimension to our faith—then the three monstrous "isms" of Utilitarianism, Materialism and Scientism would vanish from our lives, and our church would be renewed.

One of the ways to develop this "Holy" aspect to our lives is to attend Eucharistic adoration regularly and to worship at Mass with more care and reverence. At Mass, we are at the very threshold of heaven. We are in the presence of the King of Kings and Lord of Lords, surrounded by all the heavenly host. The more we realize this in our hearts, the more we will not only affirm that we believe in the "Holy" church, but we will also begin to live it in our lives.

## *How to Be Catholic*

With planes, trains and automobiles to take us everywhere in the world as fast as we can, and with modern communications that make everyone available to everyone else at any time, you would guess that more and more people would have a global or universal outlook to their lives. The opposite seems to be the case. As we are able to communicate globally and travel wherever we want, we seem to be drawing in to ourselves and our own little communities more and more.

In the first two sections of this chapter, I explored six poisonous "isms"—non-Catholic foundational beliefs which undergird the secular society in which we live. Each set of three "isms" are countered by one of the marks of the Church. So Individualism, Sentimentalism and Syncretism divide us, but being "One" with the whole church brings us into unity. The secular beliefs of Materialism, Utilitarianism and Scientism spring from the assumption that the physical world is all there is. Being aware of the "Holy" or the supernatural realm corrects the error of these three "isms" and establishes a greater dimension in our life.

The third set of "isms" that undergird our secular society is our assumption that one particular group of people or way of thinking is superior or more correct than anyone else. This assumption that "my group" is right and others are wrong leads to division in our lives, our society and our church.

The first of these three "isms" is Nationalism. This is the assumption that my ethnic group, my tribe, my clan or my country is superior. Nationalism can take a positive form in patriotism or it can manifest itself negatively in racism, militarism or extreme patriotism (my country right or wrong!). Nationalism can lead us to condone military might so that we invade other countries, convinced that we are in the right. Nationalism can blind us to our faults and to the strengths of other ethnic or national groups. Nationalism limits us to our own little clan. It not only keeps us from growing and broadening our experience, but it may also lead us to attack others in "defense" of our own tribe.

Sectarianism is like nationalism, but in the field of religion. The Sectarian first withdraws into his own comfortable little religious group. Snug in the rightness of his beliefs, he builds a fortress around himself and his religious sect. Before long, though, the false sense of security wanes and the self-righteous Sectarians start pointing the finger at others. The Sectarian mentality is, by its very nature, exclusive. The Sectarian believes he is right and everyone else is wrong. It is easy for Catholics to blame Protestants for being Sectarian, but Catholics are also prone to withdraw into special interest groups or communities within the church.

If these "isms" are sisters, then Sister Nationalism waves a flag and wears a uniform and stands up to defend her country "right or wrong." Sister Sectarian is a purse-lipped and sour old spinster who is suspicious of everyone and Sister Elitism is a haughty, well dressed, well connected snob. Both nationalism and sectarianism spring from Elitism. Elitism is the unquestioned assumption that I and my group of people are better than everybody else. Elitism can be fostered by any structure that isolates and elevates a particular group of people. The Elitist group might be a club whose members have inside knowledge, or the elite could be those who are wealthier than other people or a special group driven by a particular ideology or political ambition.

All of these "isms" display characteristics of what C. S. Lewis called The Inner Ring. This is the human tendency to identify a circle of people who are "on the inside." It is part of human ambition to be part of that "inner ring," and some people will do anything to get there. Lewis observed the insidious and perfidious nature of the "inner ring" because once one is invited to join, it turns out that within that "inner ring" of influence and power there are other "inner rings" which are increasingly more exclusive.

The tendency to Nationalism, Sectarianism and Elitism is present in our secular society, but it has crept into the Catholic Church as well. We divide into subgroups, identifying ourselves as "liberal" or "conservative." We divide among ethnic lines or we associate ourselves with a particular movement in the church or the kind of liturgy or worship that we like. There is nothing wrong with diversity of style, different forms of spirituality and different apostolates, but when they become elitist, nationalistic or sectarian, then diversity becomes division. The answer is to be more "Catholic."

One of the things I love about being a Catholic parish priest is the universality of the church. In our very ordinary American parish, we have people from every continent and ethnic group. In the congregation each Sunday, we have the young and the old, the poor and the rich, the educated and uneducated. The Catholic Church embraces all. In this universality, our Ethnic, Sectarian and Elitist divisions vanish.

Catholicism is bigger and older than all of our little groups. To be Catholic is to be Universal. The Catholic faith transcends all of our religious opinions, ethnic histories, and national cultures. We strive to be Catholic because "Catholic" transcends not just these divisions, but it also transcends time and space. It's bigger and older than all of us.

The way to treasure and live the "Catholic" aspect of our faith is to break out of our own little holy huddles, our ethnic groups and elitist mentality. We need to develop true tolerance and curiosity about others. We need to learn how to see the truth in all its different guises.

A convert friend of mine was asked why he became a Catholic and he said, "Because I wanted to belong to the Big, Holy, Old One." That was his way of saying he wanted not just to affirm his faith in the One, Holy, Catholic and Apostolic Church, but he wanted to live that faith in a practical way day by day.

## *How to Be Apostolic*

How can an ordinary Catholic be "Apostolic"? Isn't the bishop the one who is apostolic because he is a successor to the apostles? The faith is apostolic because it is handed down from the Apostles, but how can the person in the pew be "Apostolic"?

Each Sunday we say we believe in "One, Holy, Catholic and Apostolic Faith." In the three previous sections, I have outlined some underlying beliefs in our secular society that go against our Catholic faith. These false philosophies are not stated beliefs that we hold. Instead, they are a set of assumptions about the world which lie at the foundation of our worldview. They influence us in a subtle way, and they infect our Catholicism so that we have a watered-down version of our religion.

Individualism, Sentimentalism and Syncretism are the false "isms" that set up the individual as the sole authority, so they are countered by being "One." If we use the word "Holy" to signal the supernatural aspect of our faith, then being "Holy" defeats Scientism, Utilitarianism and Materialism—the three ugly sisters who stand for the assumption that there is nothing beyond the physical realm. The third set of ugly sisters includes Sectarianism, Nationalism and Elitism. These heresies set people against each other and define our faith according to our own little set of people, beliefs and customs. They are countered by the Catholic or Universal mark of the Church.

The final set of "isms" run counter to the Apostolic aspect of the Catholic faith. The first of these is Fundamentalism. We often associate "Fundamentalism" with Bible-thumping preachers in the deep South or extremist Muslim terrorists. However, "Fundamentalism" is any kind of mindset that clings to an ignorantly literal understanding of the faith. Fundamentalism distrusts scholarship, human reason and learning. Fundamentalism could also be called Fideism—a trust in personal faith alone—a trust in personal experience that is linked with a willful ignorance.

When we see this wider understanding of Fundamentalism, we can see how prevalent it is in our society. There is a trend in secular society to deliberately reject expertise, scholarship, learning, objective facts and knowledge. This Fundamentalism rejects any form of authority based on learning and expertise and prefers personal experience and emotionalism.

The second poisonous "ism" in this final set of three is Historicism. In his encyclical *Fides et Ratio*, Pope St. John Paul II defines Historicism as "the belief that the truth of a philosophy is determined on the basis of its appropriateness to a certain period and a certain historical purpose. At least implicitly therefore, the enduring validity of truth is denied. What was true in one period, historicists claim, may not be true in another."

The Historicist believes that institutions and beliefs are simply the product of the circumstances of the times in which they happened to come about. The Historicist reduces everything to the product of certain historical events, with no longer lasting truth or significance. Historicism is an insidious form of relativism. For the Historicist there is no truth that transcends all ages.

Linked with Historicism is Progressivism. Progressivism could be called the unshakeable belief in the inevitability of progress. The Progressivist believes an idea or an invention or a program is better simply because it is modern. The Progressivist believes that humans aer getting better and better simply because they have been around longer and therefore must be improving. The Progressivist's views are rooted in evolutionary theory—the conviction that all things are naturally moving to a higher and higher form of development. A reverse form of this heresy is believing that something is necessarily good not because it is new, but because it is old. Both are assumptions that undermine the Catholic faith which is, according to St. Augustine, "Ever ancient, ever new."

If these three "isms" are a set of sisters, then Fundamentalism is a dull, ignorant and emotional adolescent girl. Historicism is her cynical sophomore in college big sister who has seen it all and knows it all, while Sister Progressivist is a cheerful, naive optimist who sneers at anything old-fashioned.

These three assumptions at the foundation level of our secular society mean that many people distrust the Catholic Church without even knowing why. The Fundamentalist distrusts Catholicism because it is learned and complex. The Historicist distrusts it because it is rooted and grounded in history and a living tradition, and the Progressive hates Catholicism simply because it is ancient and authoritative.

Being "Apostolic" corrects the last three poisonous "isms." The Apostolic faith is that faith delivered to the apostles. This sacred tradition is handed on through the apostolic succession to generation after generation. The apostolic aspect of our faith corrects Fundamentalism because it demands that we use our intellects to understand, interpret and pass on the faith. Furthermore, we do not use our intellects alone, but always in harmony and submission to the whole deposit of the Apostolic faith.

Historicism is corrected by the Apostolic faith because, through the relationship of Christ to his apostles, we realize that history is not a succession of meaningless events in the past. Instead, we experience continuity from the foundations of our faith in the Hebrew religion to the Incarnation which is the center point of history, and the succession of the apostles down to this present time. This gives meaning and direction and purpose to all of history. The apostolic faith is rooted in the past and is alive in the present, and so brings rich meaning and transcendence to all moments of history.

Finally, this Apostolic faith also corrects modernism for, while it is ancient, it is also "ever new." When our faith is apostolic, we avoid the heresy of thinking a thing is good just because it is old or just because it is new. Instead, we judge it according to the Apostolic faith. Because of the Apostolic aspect of the faith, that which is ancient is forever new and that which is new is forever rooted in antiquity. The false categories of "old" and "new" become meaningless.

How can we be more "Apostolic?" By engaging our intellect. By learning more about our apostolic faith, we deepen our understanding and provide deep roots for our life and spirituality. Through the prayerful study of Scripture, the Catechism and the lives of the saints, we experience the Apostolic dimension to the faith. As we do, we are drawn into a deeper union with Christ and his Church.

# *Peter and the Papacy*

## BIBLICAL SUPPORT FOR THE PAPACY

In a world where everybody seems to have the questions, but nobody dares to have an answer, Catholics believe they do have a source for some answers. We believe Jesus had authority directly from his Father to teach the truth, and that he gave some of that authority to his apostles. Catholics believe their bishops are the successors to the Apostles and that they speak with apostolic authority.

The leader of the bishops is the Bishop of Rome—the Pope. To understand the role of the Pope we first have to see what the New Testament teaches about the apostles themselves. Once we see what the apostles were called to do, we'll see what Peter and his successors are meant to be and do.

The whole thing starts with Jesus. All Christians agree that Jesus was God's Son. He was sent to earth by God to do his will and show us what God is like. Like an ambassador or a crown prince, he came bearing the authority and power of his father, the king. In John's gospel Jesus says, "What I have spoken I have heard from my Father, and he who sent me is always with me and what I do pleases him." Jesus was sent by God, and the word "apostle" means "sent one," so Jesus—if you like—was God's apostle.

God gave Jesus power and authority so that he could fulfill his mission on earth. So in Matthew 28:18, Jesus says of himself, "All authority in heaven and on earth has been given to me," and in John 8, Jesus says that his authority and teaching are from God. Paul recognizes Jesus' divine authority as well; in Colossians 1:15–19, he says Jesus is "the image of the invisible God" and that "in him God was pleased for all his fullness and creative power to dwell." In Ephesians 1:22, Paul says God has placed all things under his feet.

So Jesus exercises God's own authority and power on earth to forgive sins, to overcome evil and to teach the truth. Now here is the amazing thing—Jesus was given this authority by God, and then in the gospels, Jesus passes along the same authority to twelve men. In Matthew 10:5 and 40, Jesus sends out the twelve saying, "He who receives you receives me, and he who receives me receives the one who sent me." After his resurrection in John's gospel, Jesus tells the apostles, "Just as God has sent me—even so I am sending you." Just as God gave Jesus power and authority to do the job, so Jesus gives these "sent ones" the power and authority to do the very same three things which he himself had authority and power to do.

In John 20:23, Jesus breathes on his apostles and says, "Receive the Holy Spirit—if you forgive the sins of any, they are forgiven; if you do not forgive them, they are not forgiven." So Jesus shares with his apostles his own authority to forgive sins. He also gives them his authority over evil. In Matthew 10:1, he calls his twelve apostles and gives them authority to drive out evil spirits and heal every kind of illness. Finally, in Matthew 28:18–20, he gives them the authority to go out into all the world and teach the truth. Then he promises to be with them to the end of the age.

It's important to see in these passages that Jesus did not give this authority and power to all of his disciples. He only gave the authority to do these things to his twelve specially chosen apostles. So God's plan was for Jesus to bear authority on earth—to forgive sins, overcome evil and teach the truth; then, just as Jesus was commissioned by God, so he commissions twelve apostles to be his agents in the world, to bear his own divine authority to forgive sins, overcome evil and teach the truth.

The apostles then passed that same authority on to their successors in the faith. They did this through the laying on of hands—or ordination. So Paul says to Timothy—his son in the faith—"do not neglect the gift you were given through the laying on of hands" (1 Timothy 4:14). This authority which the twelve apostles passed on was for the same three tasks they had been given by

Jesus himself. In the New Testament, we can see the successors of the apostles going on to do the same three acts of power which the apostles themselves were empowered to do by Jesus himself. So in 1 Timothy 4:11, Paul reminds Timothy that he was ordained to teach the truth. James 5:14–16 tells us that the elders of the church were called to exercise healing and the forgiveness of sins, and in 1 Timothy 1:3–4 Paul commands Timothy to take authority over the evil false teachers.

We have some very ancient non-Biblical writings by the second generation of Christians—men who had been taught by the apostles. This next generation after the apostles universally acknowledged that their church leaders—who the New Testament calls elders or bishops—are in the position of leadership because they received authority from the apostles. Just one quotation from an early church writer will illustrate the point. Ignatius was a church leader in Antioch—the city where the believers were first called Christians. In fact, he probably knew John and Peter when they ministered in Antioch. Ignatius travelled to Rome, where he was eventually martyred in the year 108—just forty years after Peter and Paul were martyred in Rome.

On his way, Ignatius wrote seven letters to different churches. In each one, he stresses how important it is for the Christians to obey their leaders, since they hold the authority of the apostles. So to the church at Magnesia he says, "Just as the Lord did nothing without the Father either by himself or by means of his apostles, so you must do nothing without the approval of the bishop and elders."[1] For Ignatius as for all the early Christians, the elders—that is, the bishops—have the authority to forgive sins, overcome evil and teach the truth because they were given that supernatural authority from the apostles, who in turn had received it from the Lord himself.

Furthermore, just as the bishops received the authority from the apostles, so they continued to hand that authority on to the ones who came after them. Jesus had promised that he would be with his Church to the end of time, and this is the way his authority was to be continued. So Catholics believe that this divinely appointed distribution of authority has continued down through the ages to the present day—you can actually trace the link historically. Therefore Catholics believe that their bishops—just like the bishops in the New

---

1   Ignatius of Antioch, *Epistle to the Magnesians*, 7.

Testament—are a real, dynamic and Spirit-filled link with the apostles—the sent ones of Jesus. People talk about wanting to belong to the New Testament church—if what Catholics believe is true, then the Catholic Church is the New Testament Church, alive today.

What about Peter? Did he have any special role among these twelve apostles? In the Gospels, whenever the twelve are listed, Peter comes first—and Judas last. Peter is the first apostle to whom Jesus appears after the resurrection. He is one of the small group of select apostles Jesus takes in to witness the raising of Jairus' daughter and the Transfiguration. Peter is the one who declares that Jesus is the Christ, the Son of God, and Jesus says it was by special divine revelation that Peter was able to say this. With John, Peter is the one to set up the Last Supper. At that supper, as witnessed in Luke 22:31–32, Jesus affirms Peter's importance by telling him to hold the faith, and he gives Peter a special job to strengthen his brothers in their belief.

There is more to Peter's role than simply being the leader of the twelve. When he receives the divine revelation that Jesus is the Son of God, as recorded in Matthew 16:13–20, Jesus says that this truth which Peter confesses is the rock on which the Church will be founded. Jesus then makes a pun on the name Peter—which means rock. Because he was able to receive this fundamental revelation from God, Peter himself will be the Rock on which the church is founded. That Peter—the leader of the Apostles—is the Rock on which the church is founded matches up with Paul's teaching in Ephesians 2:20 where he says the church is built on the foundation stone of the prophets and apostles.

This important passage in Matthew is full of fascinating details. For example, we're told that this conversation took place near Caesarea Philippi. At that place was a huge natural rock formation on top of which the Romans had built a temple to the pagan shepherd god Pan. So when Jesus said, "You are Peter, and on this rock I will build my church," he was looking at this great rocky foundation on which stood a pagan temple to a shepherd god. Jesus' meaning was clear—Peter, whose name means "rock," was to be the great foundation for Christ's church—the Church of the real Good Shepherd.

Peter immediately took up the leadership role in Christ's church—just as Jesus had predicted and commanded. In the first chapters of the Acts of the Apostles we see this natural leadership of Peter being exercised further. After the Ascension, Peter takes the leadership role in choosing a successor for Judas. He is the main preacher on the day of Pentecost. He is the first of the apostles to perform a miracle in Jesus' name. Peter exercises the authority to forgive sins when he calls people to repentance in Acts 2:38. In Acts 5, Peter overcomes the evil Ananias and Saphira, and we're told he cast out many demons. He is the speaker before the Jewish leaders. Peter also is the one who takes the bold step of opening the church to non-Jewish people after he is again given direct divine guidance. When he leads the church to accept non-Jewish believers he is exercising his authority to teach the truth—even when that truth seems new and controversial.

So far, we've seen that Jesus is sent by God and given God's own power and authority over all things. He shared that authority with his twelve apostles, and they in turn passed the authority to forgive sins, overcome evil, and teach the truth to their successors—the leaders of the early church. We've also seen that among the apostles Peter was not only the natural leader, but that Jesus chose him specially to be the Rock on which the church would be built. Jesus chose Peter to be spiritual equivalent of Abraham—the founding father of the people of God. He chose him to be the Prime Minister of his Kingdom, and the earthly shepherd of the flock of God. We've also seen how Peter began to do this in the Acts of the Apostles. But what happened to Peter afterwards? The New Testament doesn't tell us much about his missionary journeys and we don't have much Bible evidence about his leadership role in the city of Rome. Did Peter really end up as the leader of the Roman church? Catholics believe he was not only the leader of the Roman church, but that the leaders who followed him were the successors of his special commission from Jesus to lead the flock of God.

Peter was obviously in charge when he stood up to preach the first Spirit-filled sermon at Pentecost. We know that he set out from Jerusalem on missionary journeys. But then the book of Acts shifts its attention from Peter to Paul. This was because Acts was written by Luke, who was a companion of Paul. So where else can we get information about what happened to Peter?

First of all, there is the rest of the New Testament itself. Most scholars agree that the first letter of Peter was written by Peter. In 1 Peter 5:13, we find that Peter is writing from a place he calls "Babylon." From the book of Revelation, we know that "Babylon" is an early Christian code word for the city of Rome. The First letter of Peter tells us a good deal about the situation at that time—about thirty years after Jesus' death and resurrection. The church was established in Rome, and Paul was also ministering there. From Rome Peter writes to churches throughout Asia Minor—what is now Turkey.

The letters from Peter to these churches suggests that Peter went to them on his missionary journeys. The Scriptural evidence is also backed up by the historians of the early church. Clement of Alexandria lived about one hundred years after Peter's death and looking back to much older accounts, he records how the Gospel of Mark came to be written down. He says,

> After Peter had announced the Word of God in Rome and preached the gospel in the spirit of God, the multitude of hearers requested Mark, who had long accompanied Peter on all his journeys, to write down what the Apostles had preached to them.[2]

Other earlier writers Papias and Irenaeus also record the fact that Peter and Mark—his "son in the faith"—ended up in Rome and that the Gospel of Mark was written there, and was based on Peter's preaching and eyewitness accounts.

What else can we reconstruct to get a picture of the early church in the city of Rome during Peter's lifetime? The church was an underground movement. We know from 2 Tim. 4:13 that Paul himself was in chains in a damp prison. Peter probably kept on the move, visiting outlying churches, and meeting in the homes of the Christians for secret worship. In fact, many inscriptions on the walls of an ancient house in Rome called the House of Hermes, excavated in 1915, indicate that Peter used that very house as a center of his ministry. While there are scraps of evidence which tell us what the church was like, in fact we have very little written evidence about the church from those earliest days. The reason so little exists is that the systematic persecution of the church over the next two hundred years included the widespread destruction of all the Christian holy writings. When the Christians weren't actually being thrown to the wild beasts, their property was confiscated, their books were burnt and their worship disrupted.

Nevertheless, the historians and writers of the church who lived just following the time of the apostles did record that Peter and Paul lived in Rome. They recorded that both met their death in the terrible persecutions of Nero around A.D. 65; that Paul was beheaded and Peter crucified upside

---

2 As quoted in Eusebius, *Ecclesiastical History*, 4.4.

down. They also record that both Peter and Paul were buried in Rome. In fact, when Christianity became legal in 315, the Emperor Constantine built the first basilica of Peter on the traditional site of Peter's tomb. In the mid-20th century, excavations under the great church of St. Peter in Rome uncovered a first century tomb which many believe is the actual tomb of Peter himself.

So Peter ended his earthly life in the city of Rome. Along with Paul, he must have been the leader of the infant Roman church. But what happened next? What about those who came after him? We've already seen that the apostles passed on their authority to the church leaders they appointed in various places. So in the New Testament Paul appoints Titus as the church leader for Cyprus and tells him to select and appoint other church elders; and in his first epistle Peter addresses the elders in the various churches he founded as 'his fellow shepherds,' that is, those with whom he shared his Christ-given role of earthly shepherd of the flock of God.

But what did the Christians in Rome think about their leaders during the years just after the apostles died?

We have one very important document from those early years just after the death of the apostles. The letter is from a church leader in Rome called Clement. A Roman Christian named Clement is actually mentioned in chapter four of Paul's letter to the Philippians—a letter which was written from Rome. There Paul refers to Clement as a fellow worker. It could be the same Clement who wrote a letter to the Church at Corinth about the year 95—just thirty years after Peter's death. In the letter, Clement tells how the apostles travelled around and appointed new leaders who bore the same authority they had received from the Lord himself. Listen to what this voice says, and remember that it was written by someone who may have been taught by the apostles themselves. Clement says, "Now the Gospel was given to the Apostles for us by the Lord Jesus Christ; and Jesus Christ was sent from God. That is to say, Christ received his commission from God and the Apostles theirs from Christ."[3] Later in the letter, he claims Peter and Paul as the apostles of the Roman church and goes on to say,

> Our apostles also knew through our Lord Jesus Christ, that there would be strife on the question of the bishop's office. Therefore, for

---

3   *1 Clement*, 42.

this reason, since they had complete foreknowledge, they appointed the aforesaid persons and later made further provision that if they should fall asleep, other tested men should succeed to their ministry.[4]

Because the question of leadership was important, the Christians in Rome were careful to record who their own leaders were after Peter and Paul were killed. So we have a list of the first leaders of the Roman church after Peter. The list says that a man called Linus was the next leader after Peter. A person with this name appears in 2 Timothy 4:21. This epistle was written from Paul's prison in Rome, and Paul says to Timothy that Linus sends greetings. The second leader after Peter was Cletus, about whom we know very little. The third man was Clement—the one who wrote the famous letter to the Church at Corinth, and who may also have been mentioned by Paul.

These documents show us that Peter—the one Jesus appointed as leader of the apostles—did end up in Rome, and that he was the leader of the church there. These early writings also tell us that the apostles appointed successors in the different churches, and that the successors were considered the rightful inheritors of the apostolic authority—an authority given to them directly by Jesus.

Peter may have been the leader of the Apostles, and he may have ended up as the leader of the Church of Rome, but does that mean he was considered leader of the whole church? And did his successors as the leader of the Roman Church continue to be seen as the leaders of the whole church? If so, then we can see how the idea that the Bishop of Rome continues to be the Prime Minister of Christ's Kingdom on earth might have developed. Jesus commanded Peter to be in charge of his flock as the head pastor in his place, but did that job of overall leadership pass on to those who stepped into Peter's shoes?

Even Paul tells us in Gal. 1:18 and 2:22 that he went to Peter to validate his own teaching and authority. We know that Peter took on missionary travels, and we know from his epistles—written from Rome—that he felt confident to write authoritatively to Christians throughout the known world. In other words, even in his lifetime, Peter, based in Rome, was the spokesman and leader of the whole church.

This authority of the Roman Church over other churches continued after

---

4    *1 Clement* 44.1–2.

Peter's death. The letter of Clement was written from Rome to the church at Corinth. Just thirty years after Peter's death, Clement speaks for the elders of the Roman church when he calls the Corinthian church into order and exercises authority over them. Writing just sixty years later, Irenaeus, a French bishop who had studied in Rome says,

> Those who wish to see the truth can observe in every church the tradition of the Apostles made manifest in the whole world . . . therefore we refute those who hold unauthorized assemblies . . . by pointing to the greatest and oldest church, a church known to all men, which was founded and established at Rome by the most renowned Apostles Peter and Paul . . . . For it is a matter of necessity that with this Church, on account of its preeminent authority, every Church should agree, that is, the faithful everywhere, inasmuch as in her the apostolic tradition has been preserved continuously by those who are everywhere.[5]

Down through the ages many men have stood in the shoes of Peter as Bishop of Rome. Some have been saints, some have been sinners. The vast majority have been hard-working, prayerful and dedicated leaders of Christ's church. But one of the amazing things which scholars tell us about the Popes is that not once have the bishops of Rome taught heresy. Other bishops have fallen into error, and the Bishops of Rome have brought them back to the truth. The Popes haven't all been angels; some have been very wicked indeed. Peter himself denied the Lord three times. But despite their human failings, they have led the whole Christian church in proclaiming the unfailing gospel of Jesus Christ. They did so in the footsteps of Peter—that amazing man Jesus called to continue his work on earth. The one whose name means "rock." The one who was called to become the father of the people of God. The one whose life and teaching remains the foundation of Christ's Church.

---

5   Irenaeus, *Against Heresies*, 3.3.2.

An Answer *Not* An Argument / Fr. Dwight Longenecker

# COME ROCK! COME ROPE!

When I was in the Bible doctrine class at Bob Jones University, we had to memorize verses from the Bible that proved the doctrines we were studying. I don't regret it. Those wonderful passages of Scripture still echo in my mind and heart today. One of the verses we had to memorize was Matthew 16:18: "I tell you that you are Peter, and on this rock I will build my church and the gates of hell will not prevail against it."

While a Catholic college student might memorize this verse to prove his beliefs about the papacy, we actually learned it in order to deny Catholic beliefs about the papacy. It was explained that the "rock" in this verse was not Peter, but his profession of faith that Jesus Christ was the Son of God. Christ's pun on the name "Peter-*petros*" was not a pun at all because "*petros*" meant little stone, and therefore Jesus could not have intended the "rock" to be Peter, because he was speaking of a foundation stone. Only many years later did I begin to reassess the teaching I had received about this famous and important verse.

The fundamentalists protested that Catholics built the entire edifice of papal authority on this one verse taken out of context, and that this was a misuse of Scripture. An important doctrine, they said, should not be developed on one proof text alone. In fact, they are right, but as I began to study the Catholic faith more openly, I came to understand that the Catholic Church does not rely on this one verse alone to support papal claims. She takes the verse in the entire fullness of its context.

Instead of just one proof text, there are three important Biblical images, Rock, Steward and Shepherd, that come together to support the Catholic Church's claims to papal authority. These three images are not just in one verse, but are rooted in the Old Testament and affirmed in the New. Like a strong, three-strand, braided rope, the three images of Rock, Steward and Shepherd provide a powerful interlocking and interdependent support for the authority Christ intended to leave with his Church on Earth.

## *The Old Testament Rock*

A word study of the Old Testament shows the importance of the Rock as an image of foundational authority and strength. In Genesis 49:24 the patriarch Jacob is blessing his sons and he says that Joseph's arm is strong in battle because it is upheld by "the Shepherd, the Rock of Israel." The Shepherd and the Rock are symbols of God's solid care and loving support for his people.

For Moses, the Rock is a solid place to stand and a secure hiding place (Ex. 33:21–22). For the people of Israel the rock is a miraculous source of refreshment and life (Ex. 17:6). Throughout the book of Deuteronomy, the Lord is a Rock who is perfect and one who fathers his children and provides an abundant life for them (Dt. 32:4, 13, 15, 18).

The great psalmist King David refers time and again to the Lord as his rock, his fortress and his deliverer (2 Sam. 22:2; Ps. 18, 19 et al.) In a beautiful image, the psalmist praises God for lifting his feet from the miry clay and setting them firm upon a rock (Ps. 40:2). Throughout the psalms the Rock becomes a predominant image for the solid, secure and trustworthy Lord of Israel.

The prophet Isaiah echoes the psalmist. For him too, the Lord is the Rock. Shelter is found in the shadow of a rock in a dry and thirsty land (Isa. 32:2). God is likened to the "Rock eternal" (Isa. 26:4) and the Lord is the rock from which the people of Israel are hewn (Isa. 51:1). Habakkuk reaffirms that the Lord is the Rock (Hab. 1:12). At the end of the Old Testament, the prophet Zechariah says that God will make Jerusalem an immoveable rock for all nations (Zech. 12:3).

## *New Testament Rock*

In the Old Testament, the powerful image of the rock repeatedly refers to God himself. In the New Testament, St. Paul unlocks the image of the rock and says clearly that the foundation stone is Jesus Christ himself (Rom. 9:33; 1 Cor. 10:4). The incarnate Christ is therefore the manifestation of the Rock who is God. He therefore has the authority to name someone who will share his rock-like status.

It is within the whole Old Testament context that Jesus the Rock gives his teaching about the Rock. In the important passage of Isaiah 51, God is the "rock from which the people of Israel are hewn, but they are told to "look to Abraham your father and to Sarah who gave you birth." In notes 51 and

52 in Stephen Ray's masterful work *Upon This Rock*,[1] evidence is piled up showing that the Jewish teachers repeatedly referred to Abraham as the God-appointed foundation stone of the Jewish people. God was the ultimate Rock, but Abraham was his earthly presence. Just as Abram was given a new name to indicate his new foundational status, so Jesus gives Simon a new name "Rock" to indicate his foundational status in the new covenant.

## *King, Keys and the Royal Steward*

The second strand in the braided rope of Petrine authority is the image of Steward. The steward in a royal household is a personage met throughout the Old Testament record. The patriarch Joseph works as a steward in the palace in Egypt. King Saul also has a steward, as does the prince Mephibosheth. But for understanding of Matthew 16:19–22, the most important image of steward in the Old Testament is in Isaiah 22.

In Isaiah 22, the prophet is foretelling the fall of one royal steward and the succession of another. Shebna is being replaced by Eliakim, and the prophet says to the rejected Shebna (Isa. 22:21–22),

> I will clothe him with your robe and fasten your sash around him and hand your authority over to him. He will be a father to those who live in Jerusalem and to the house of Judah. I will place on his shoulder the key to the house of David; what he opens no one can shut, and what he shuts no one can open.

The true holder of the keys to the kingdom is the king himself. In the Book of Revelation, we see that the risen and glorified Christ holds the power of the keys—the power to bind and loose. John has a vision of Christ who says, "I am the First and the Last. I am the Living One; I was dead, and behold I am alive for ever and ever! And I hold the keys of death and Hades" (Rev. 1:18).

So the king holds the keys of the kingdom, but he delegates his power to the steward. The keys of the kingdom are the symbol of this delegated authority. The keys not only opened all the doors, but they provided access to the storehouses and financial resources of the king. In addition, the keys of the kingdom were worn on a sash that was a ceremonial badge of office. The

---

1 Stephen K. Ray, *Upon This Rock* (Ignatius Press, 2009).

passage and the customs all reveal that the royal steward held an office given by the king, and that it was a successive office—the keys being handed to the next steward as a sign of the continuing delegated authority of the king himself.

This is the Old Testament setting that Jesus' disciples would have understood completely as he quoted this particular passage in Matthew 16. When Jesus said to Peter, "I will give you the keys of the kingdom of heaven; whatever you bind on earth will be bound in heaven, and whatever you loose on earth will be loosed in heaven," his disciples would have not only recognized the passage from Isaiah. They would also have understood that not only was Jesus calling himself the King of his kingdom, he was appointing Peter as his royal steward. That the ascended and glorified Christ is seen by John to hold the eternal keys only confirms the intention of Jesus to delegate that power to Peter—the foundation stone of his Church.

That Matthew 16:17–19 is a direct quotation from Isaiah 22 is an interpretation held both by Catholic scholars and by a number of Protestant Biblical scholars. Stephen Ray in his book *Upon This Rock*,[2] shows by quotation that many Protestant scholars too support this understanding and affirm that Jesus is delegating his authority over life and death, heaven and hell to the founder of his church on earth.

## *The Good Shepherd*

The third strand in the strong rope of Scriptural support for papal authority is the image of the Good Shepherd. This powerful image is so abundant in the Old Testament that there is no room in this short article to even begin to recount all the references. Suffice it to say that the Hebrew people were a nomadic shepherd people. The image of the lamb and the shepherd are woven in and through their story at every glance, and from the beginning God himself is seen to be the shepherd of his people.

In Genesis 48 the old man Jacob, before blessing his sons, says that the Lord God of his fathers has been his Shepherd his whole life long. The prophet Micah sees the people of Israel as "sheep without a shepherd." The Shepherd King David calls the Lord his shepherd (Ps. 23 et al). The prophet Isaiah says

---

[2] Stephen K. Ray, *Upon This Rock* (Ignatius Press, 2009), nn. 47–49.

that the Sovereign Lord will "tend his flock like a shepherd: He gathers the lambs in his arms, and carries them close to his heart; he gently leads those that have young" (Isa. 40:11).

In the Book of Jeremiah, the prophet rages against the corrupt leadership of the people of Israel, calling the leaders wicked and abusive shepherds, but the theme of the Lord as the Good Shepherd reaches its Old Testament climax in the Book of Ezekiel. There God promises that he himself will be the shepherd of his people Israel. So the Lord says in Ezekiel (Ez. 34:12, 16):

> As a shepherd looks after his scattered flock when he is with them, so will I look after my sheep. I will rescue them from all the places where they were scattered on a day of clouds and darkness . . . . I will search for the lost and bring back the strays. I will bind up the injured and strengthen the weak, but the sleek and the strong I will destroy. I will shepherd the flock with justice.

Finally, the Lord's servant, the Son of David, will come and be the shepherd of the lost flock (Ez. 34:22–24):

> I will save my flock, and they will no longer be plundered. I will judge between one sheep and another. I will place over them one shepherd, my servant David, and he will tend them; he will tend them and be their shepherd. I the LORD will be their God, and my servant David will be prince among them.

## *Christ the Good Shepherd*

One of the clearest signs, therefore, of Christ's self-knowledge as the Son of God is given when he calls himself the Good Shepherd. In story after story, Jesus uses the image of the Good Shepherd to refer to his own ministry. He explicitly calls himself the Good Shepherd (Jn. 10:11, 14) who has come to the lost sheep of the house of Israel (Mt. 15:24) and tells the story of the lost sheep placing himself in the story as the Divine Shepherd who fulfills Ezekiel's prophecy of seeking the lost sheep (Lk. 15). The author of the Book of Hebrews calls Christ the Great Shepherd of the Sheep (Heb. 13:20). Peter calls Jesus the Shepherd and overseer of souls (1 Pt. 2:25). In the Book of Revelation, the lamb on the throne is also the shepherd of the lost souls (Rev. 7:17).

When Jesus Christ after his resurrection solemnly instructs Peter to "feed my lambs, watch over my sheep, and feed my sheep" (Jn. 21:15–17), the ramifications are enormous. Throughout the Old Testament, God himself is understood to be the Good Shepherd. He promises to come and be the shepherd of his people. This will be done through his servant David. When Jesus Christ the Son of David fulfills this prophecy, all is complete. Before he returns to heaven he gives this astounding command for Peter to take charge of his pastoral ministry. Now Peter is to take on the role of Good Shepherd in Christ's place.

## *The Vicar of Christ*

When I was an Anglican priest in England I held the title of "vicar" of the parish. The term was derived from the fact that the vicar was a priest appointed to do a job in the stead of the man who was the official parish priest. One priest might oversee various parishes, and so he appointed vicars to do the job when he couldn't be there.

Many non-Catholic Christians object to the Pope being called "the Vicar of Christ." But the word "vicar" simply stands for one who vicariously stands in for another person. A "vicar" is someone to whom a job is delegated. The three strands of Biblical imagery: Rock, Steward and Shepherd show in three different ways that Jesus intended Peter to exercise his ministry and authority here on earth.

The fact that there are three images is important, because the number three was considered by Biblical writers to be one of the perfect numbers. A statement was most authoritative when it was expressed three times in three different ways.

We see this in the passage in John 21. Jesus gives his pastoral authority to Peter with three solemn commands: "Feed my lambs, take care of my sheep, feed my sheep." This passage combines Jesus' delegation of his authority three different times in three different ways. He uses imagery that is packed into the Old Testament in dozens of instances throughout the whole Old Testament witness. Jesus' delegation of authority to Peter is therefore overwhelmingly clear.

## A Successive Ministry

"Ah yes," the reluctant non-Catholic will protest, "but there is no evidence that this ministry will be successive." However, the whole context and meaning of the imagery from the beginning to the end show it to be a ministry that must be successive.

First of all, the image of the rock is, by its very nature, a timeless and everlasting image. That's why the image of the rock was chosen. That's what rocks are. They're there to stay. Then, in Matthew 16, Jesus himself says that the steward's ministry will have an eternal dimension. He holds the keys to the Kingdom of God and the gates of hell will never prevail against it. Finally, the image of the Shepherd, as we have seen, is an eternal one because God himself is the ultimate Good Shepherd. If the rock, the steward and the Shepherd are eternal ministries, then for it to last that long the ministry must be successive. How could this eternal ministry have died out with Peter himself and still been eternal?

History shows that from the earliest days the Christians considered Peter to be the very Rock, Steward and Shepherd that Jesus proclaimed him to be. Furthermore, from the earliest days, they considered his successor to be the Bishop of Rome. Today that Bishop of Rome lives as the Rock, the Steward and the Shepherd just a few hundred yards from the site of Peter's death and burial.

Does the Catholic Church build the claims to papal authority on one verse taken out of context? Hardly. The three strands of Rock, Steward and Shepherd are woven in and through the whole of Scripture, coming into focus in the life of Jesus Christ who is the true Rock, the King of the Kingdom and Good Shepherd, and who hands his authority on earth to Peter until he comes again.

## Assuming Infallibility

There's a scene in *Brideshead Revisited* in which the worldly but spiritually ignorant Rex Mottram is receiving instruction in the Catholic faith. Father Mowbray recounts how he was unable to explain the dogma of papal infallibility to Rex,

> Then again I asked him: "Supposing the Pope looked up and saw a cloud and said 'It's going to rain', would that be bound to happen?"

"Oh, yes, Father." "But supposing it didn't?" He thought a moment and said, "I suppose it would be sort of raining spiritually, only we were too sinful to see it."

Similar confusion exists in the popular mind concerning papal infallibility and, unfortunately, the dogma continues to confound many Catholics. There are Catholics who believe whatever a pope says must be divinely inspired, and if it is not exactly infallible it should be treated as such. It is amazing how this "high" view of papal authority suddenly appears among certain Catholics when the current pope happens to be agreeable to them. Thus, liberal Catholics, who for years consistently mocked, ignored and dismissed Pope St. John Paul II and Pope Benedict, have suddenly become (with Pope Francis) staunch defenders of papal infallibility. Likewise, some conservatives who took a high view of papal authority under Popes John Paul and Benedict, have discovered that they are much more open-minded since the ascent of Cardinal Bergoglio to the throne of Peter.

It is worthwhile for all Catholics to be reminded of the extent and limits of the dogma of papal infallibility. Defined at the first Vatican Council, the dogma states that in virtue of the promise of Jesus to Peter, the Pope is preserved from the possibility of error "[w]hen, in the exercise of his office as shepherd and teacher of all Christians, in virtue of his supreme apostolic authority, he defines a doctrine concerning faith or morals to be held by the whole Church."[3] Many have observed that rather than extending papal power and privilege, the definition decreases papal authority by strict imposing limits and conditions.

First, the pope himself must make the statement. Secondly, he must be speaking "*ex cathedra*" or "from the chair of Peter." In other words, as supreme teacher and shepherd he must be consciously making a formal papal decree. Thirdly, he must be defining a doctrine. He is not expressing an opinion or musing about current events. He is making a decision and clarifying what was previously debated. Fourth, the teaching must be about faith and morals, and fifth, the decree must be vital for the fullness of the faith for the whole church universal.

Therefore, it is very rare that a pope speaks infallibly. Aside from canonizations, only one such statement, the 1950 decree concerning the

---

[3] *Pastor Aeternus*, 4.9.

Assumption of Mary, has been proclaimed since 1870. Popes themselves have reminded us of this fact. Pope Benedict XVI said, "The Pope is not an oracle; he is infallible in very rare situations."[4] Pope John XXIII quipped, "I am only infallible if I speak infallibly but I shall never do that, so I am not infallible."[5]

A good illustration of how papal infallibility actually works is in the comparatively recent definition of the Assumption of the Blessed Virgin Mary. The Assumption was a pious doctrine that had been believed in the church from early days. The first written accounts date from the fourth and fifth centuries, but in both the Eastern and Western church the tradition and devotions developed, so that by the modern age the Assumption (or Dormition) of the Virgin was a universally celebrated feast.

What is interesting is how Pope Pius XII exercised his infallible authority. He did not wake up one morning, yawn and say, "I think I'll define the dogma of the Assumption today." In November 1950, he defined the dogma in his decree, *Munificentissimus Deus*, but this was preceded by years of deliberation, starting in 1946 when he sent an encyclical letter, *Deiparae Virginis Mariae*, to all the bishops of the church.

In that encyclical, Pius XII pointed out that for a long time past, numerous petitions had been received,

> [from] cardinals, patriarchs, archbishops, bishops, priests, religious of both sexes, associations, universities and innumerable private persons, all begging that the bodily Assumption into heaven of the Blessed Virgin should be defined and proclaimed as a dogma of faith.[6]

Furthermore, the definition had also been requested by the fathers of the First Vatican Council. Therefore, the pope asked all bishops for their opinion. Not only that, he asked them to consult with the faithful:

> We earnestly beg you to inform us about the devotion of your clergy and people (taking into account their faith and piety) toward the Assumption of the most Blessed Virgin Mary. More especially We wish to know if you, Venerable Brethren, with your learning and prudence consider that the bodily Assumption of the Immaculate Blessed Virgin

---

4 "Pope Has No Easy 'Recipe' for Church Crisis." *Zenit*, 29 July 2005.
5 John XXIII, Audience at the Greek College in Rome.
6 Pius XII, *Deiparae Virginis Mariae*, 2.

can be proposed and defined as a dogma of faith, and whether in addition to your own wishes this is desired by your clergy and people.[7]

As a convert to the Catholic faith, when I first learned of this I was astounded. Rather like Rex Mottram, I assumed that papal infallibility was an example of Roman Catholic arrogance and overreaching papal power. Instead, the infallible definition of a dogma was the final seal on a process that had taken centuries to mature. The pope's infallible definition of a dogma was also a response to grassroots requests and the result of a conscious and complete consultation process not only with the bishops and theologians, but with all the clergy and faithful. I was impressed.

The carefully worded definition of papal infallibility therefore has to be understood alongside the actual practice of papal infallibility. It is true that the pope can act unilaterally and infallibly, but in practice he only exercises his infallible charism in unity with the college of bishops, consistently with the whole teaching of the church, and in union with the Sacred Scriptures and Sacred Tradition.

What is the proper response of the faithful to the teaching authority of the pope? Regarding infallibly-declared dogmas, we are to give "the obedience of faith."[8] Hence as Pope Pius XII solemnly stated after defining the dogma, "If anyone . . . should dare willfully to deny or to call into doubt that which we have defined, let him know that he has fallen away completely from the divine and Catholic Faith." The *Catechism of the Catholic Church* reminds us that we are to embrace other church teachings with "religious assent."[9]

Does papal infallibility demand unthinking subservience in all things? No. We are expected to be intellectually engaged in our faith. We might personally dislike a particular pope. We might find certain papal teachings or statements challenging. We may question a pope's judgements and offer a critique of his opinions, but we must always do so in a quest to understand and obey more fully. What a good Catholic cannot do is disrespect a pope, disregard his teaching and dismiss his authority in a spirit of rebellion and dissent.

---

7   Pius XII, *Deiparae Virginis Mariae* 4.
8   *Catechism of the Catholic Church*, 891.
9   *Catechism of the Catholic Church*, 892.

## *THE TRAIL OF BLOOD* AND THE EARLY PAPACY

Some time ago an acquaintance from my days as a fundamentalist sent me an email. Kevin had become a Baptist pastor and was disappointed that I had been "deceived by the Catholic Church." He wanted to know my reasons for becoming Catholic.

I get such emails from time to time, and rather than get involved in arguments about purgatory or candles or Mary worship or indulgences, I usually cut straight to the point and try to engage my correspondent with the question of authority in the Church.

Kevin told me that to follow the Pope was an ancient error, and when I asked where he got his authority, he promised to send me a book called *The Trail of Blood*.[1] Written by a Baptist pastor named J. M. Carroll, this book asserts that Baptists are not really Protestants because they never broke away from the Catholic Church. Instead they are part of an ancient line of "true and faithful Biblical Christians," dating right back through the Waldensians and Henricians to the Cathars, the Novatians, Montanists and eventually John the Baptist. This view is called Baptist Successionism or Landmarkism. It is also taught by John T. Christian in his book, *A History of the Baptists*.[2]

Baptist Successionism is a theory more theological than historical. For the proponents, the fact that there is no historical proof for their theory simply shows how good the Catholic Church was at persecution and cover-up. Baptist Successionism can never be disproved, because all that is required for their succession to be transmitted was a small group of faithful people somewhere at some time who kept the flame of the true faith alive. The authors of this rather fictional history skim happily over the heretical beliefs of their supposed forefathers in the faith. It is sufficient for them that all these groups were opposed to, and persecuted by, the Catholics.

Most educated Evangelicals would snicker at such bogus scholarship. In

---

[1] J. M. Carroll, *The Trail of Blood: Following the Christians Down through the Centuries, or The History of Baptist Churches From the Time of Christ, Their Founder, to the Present Day* (Lexington, Kentucky: Ashland Avenue Baptist Church, 1931).

[2] John T. Christian, *A History of the Baptists*, 2 vols. (Sunday School Board of The Southern Baptist Convention, 1922).

fact, many Evangelicals are totally ignorant of the works of J. M. Carroll and the arcane historical theories of Baptist Successionism. Nevertheless, the basic assumptions of Baptist Successionism provide the foundation for most current independent Baptist explanations of early Church history. These assumptions are the foundation for the typical independent Baptist understanding (or misunderstanding) of the Church. The assumptions about the early church are these: 1) Jesus Christ never intended such a thing as a monarchical papacy; 2) The church of the New Testament age was decentralized; 3) The early church was essentially local and congregational in government; 4) The church became hierarchical after the conversion of Constantine in the fourth century; and 5) the papacy was invented by Pope Leo the Great, who reigned from 440–460.

## *Just the Facts*

These five basic assumptions that the typical Evangelical holds about the papacy are part of the wallpaper in the Evangelical world. Being brought up in an independent Bible Church, I was taught that our little fellowship of Christians meeting to study the Bible, pray and sing gospel songs was like the "early Christians" meeting in their house churches. I had a mental picture of the "Catholic Pope" which I had pieced together from a whole range of biased sources. When I heard the word "pope" I pictured a corpulent Italian with the juicy name "Borgia" who drank a lot of wine, and who was supposed to be celibate, but who not only had mistresses, but sons who he called "nephews." This "pope" had big banquets in one of his many palaces, was very rich, rode out to war when he felt like it and liked to tell Michelangelo how to paint. Part of the whole colorful story was the idea that there had never been anything like this "pope" until the office was later invented by the corrupt Catholic Church.

But of course, the idea that the florid Renaissance pope is typical of all popes is not a Catholic invention, but a Protestant one. Protestantism has been compelled to rewrite all history according to its own necessities. In the oft-quoted words of French historian Augustin Thierry, "To live, Protestantism found itself forced to build up a history of its own."

The five basic assumptions of non-Catholic Christians can be corrected by looking at the history of the early church. Did Jesus envision and plan a monarchical papacy? Was the early church decentralized? Was the early church essentially local and congregational? Did the early church only become hierarchical after the emperor was converted? Did Leo the Great invent the papacy in the fifth century? To examine this we'll have to put off to one side the preconceptions and mental images of Borgia popes and get down to "just the facts, ma'am."

## Did Jesus Plan a Monarchical Papacy?

Jesus certainly did not plan for the inflated and corrupt popes of the popular imagination. He intended to found a church, but the church was not democratic in structure. It was established with a clear concept of leadership by an individual. In Matthew 16:18–19, Jesus says to Simon Peter, "You are Peter, and on this Rock I will build my church, and the gates of Hell will not overcome it." So, Jesus established his church not on a congregational model, but on the model of personal leadership.

Was this a monarchical papacy? In a way it was. In Matthew 16, Jesus goes on to say to Peter, "I will give you the keys of the kingdom of heaven; whatever you bind on earth will be bound in heaven, and whatever you loose on earth will be loosed in heaven." This is a direct reference back to Isaiah 22:22, where the prophet recognizes Eliakim as the steward of the royal House of David. The steward was the Prime Minister of the Kingdom. The keys of the kingdom were the sign of his personal authority delegated by the king himself. Jesus never intended a monarchical papacy in the corrupt sense of the Pope being an absolute worldly monarch, but the church leadership Jesus intended was "monarchical" in the sense that it was based on his authority as King of Kings.

The reference to Isaiah 22 shows that the structure of Jesus' kingdom was modeled on King David's dynastic court. In Luke 1:32–33, Jesus' birth is announced in royal terms. He will inherit the throne of his father David. He will rule over the house of Jacob and his kingdom shall never end. Like Eliakim, to whom Jesus refers, Peter is to be the appointed authority in this court, and as such his role is that of steward and ruler in the absence of the High King, the scion of the House of David. That Peter assumes this pre-eminent role of leadership in the early church is attested to throughout the New Testament from his first place in the list of the apostles, to his dynamic preaching on the day of Pentecost, his decision making at the Council of Jerusalem and the deference shown to him by St. Paul and the other apostles.

Did Jesus plan the monarchical papacy? He did not plan for the corrupt, venal and worldly papacy that it has sometimes become down through history, but Jesus did plan for one man to be his royal delegate on earth. He did plan for one man to lead the others (Lk. 22:32) He did plan for one man to take up the spiritual and temporal leadership of his church. This is shown not only through the famous passage from Matthew 16, but also in the final chapter of John's gospel where Jesus the Good Shepherd hands his pastoral role over to Peter.

## *Was the early church decentralized?*

Independent Evangelical churches follow the Baptist Successionist idea that the early church was decentralized. They like to imagine that the early Christians met in their homes for Bible study and prayer, and that in this pure form they existed independently of any central authority. It is easy to imagine that long ago in the ancient world, transportation must have been difficult and communication rare, so that no form of centralized church authority could have existed even if it had been desirable.

The most straightforward reading of the Acts of the Apostles shows this to be untrue. A further reading of other early church documents confirms that this is no more than a back-projected invention. In the Acts of the Apostles what we find is a church that is immediately centralized in Jerusalem. When Peter has his disturbing vision in which God directs him to admit the Gentiles to the Church, he does not decide this issue on his own, but instead immediately refers it back to the entire apostolic leadership in Jerusalem (Acts 11:2).

The mission of the infant church was directed from Jerusalem, with Barnabas and Agabus being sent to Antioch (Acts 11:22, 27) The Council of Jerusalem (Acts 15) was convened to decide on the Gentile issue, and a letter of instruction was sent to the new churches in Antioch, Syria and Cilicia (Acts 15:23). We see Philip, John Mark, Barnabas and Paul traveling to and from Jerusalem and providing a teaching and disciplinary link from the new churches back to the centralized church in Jerusalem.

After the martyrdom of James, the leadership shifts to Peter and Paul. The authority is not centered on Jerusalem, but through the epistles of Peter and

Paul to the various churches, we see a centralized authority that is vested in those two apostles. This central authority was very soon focused on Rome, so that St. Ignatius, a bishop of the church in Antioch, would write to the Romans in the year 108 affirming that their church was the one that had the "superior place in love among the churches."[3]

Historian Eamon Duffy suggests that the earliest leadership in the Roman church may have been more conciliar than monarchical because in his letter to the Corinthians, Clement of Rome doesn't write as the Bishop of Rome. Even if this is so, though, Duffy confirms that the early church believed Clement was the fourth Bishop of Rome and understood Clement's letter as supporting centralized Roman authority. He also concedes that by the time of Irenaeus in the mid-second century, the centralizing role of the Bishop of Rome was already well established. From then on, citation after citation from the apostolic Fathers can be compiled to show that the whole church from Gaul to North Africa and from Syria to Spain affirmed the primacy of the Bishop of Rome as the successor of Peter and Paul.[4]

The acceptance of this centralized authority was a sign of belonging to the one true Church. St. Jerome could therefore write to Pope Damasus in the mid-300s,

> I think it is my duty to consult the chair of Peter, and to turn to a church whose faith has been praised by Paul . . . . My words are spoken to the successor of the fisherman, to the disciple of the cross. As I follow no leader save Christ, so I communicate with none but your blessedness, that is, with the chair of Peter. For this, I know, is the rock on which the church is built![5]

## *Was the Early Church Local and Congregational?*

We find no evidence of a network of independent, local churches ruled democratically by individual congregations. Instead, from the beginning we find the churches ruled by elders (bishops). So in the New Testament, we

---

3   Ignatius of Antioch, *Letter to the Romans*.

4   Eamon Duffy, *Saints and Sinners: A History of the Popes*, 3rd ed. (New Haven, Conn. London: Yale University Press, 2006), 9–16.

5   Jerome, *Letter 15*, 2.

find the apostles appointing elders in the churches (Acts 14:23; Titus 1:5). The elders kept in touch with the apostles and with the elders of the other churches through travel and communication by epistle (1Pt. 1:1; 5:1).

Nor do we find in the early church evidence of independent congregations meeting on their own and determining their own affairs by reading the Bible. We have to remember that in the first two centuries there was no Bible as such anyway: the canon of the New Testament had not yet been decided. Instead, from the earliest time we find churches ruled by the bishops and clergy whose authenticity is validated by their succession from the apostles. So Clement of Rome writes,

> Our apostles also knew, through our Lord Jesus Christ, that there would be strife on the question of the bishop's office. Therefore for this reason . . . they appointed the aforesaid persons and later made further provision that if they should fall asleep other tested men should succeed to their ministry.[6]

Ignatius of Antioch in Syria writes letters to six different churches and instructs the Romans, "be submissive to the bishop and to one another as Jesus Christ was to the Father and the Apostles to Christ . . . that there may be unity."[7]

This apostolic ministry was present in each city, but centralized in Rome. The idea of a church being independent, local and congregational is rejected. It serves here to quote again the passage from the late second century bishop Irenaeus, as he writes,

> Those who wish to see the truth can observe in every church the tradition of the Apostles made manifest in the whole world . . . therefore we refute those who hold unauthorized assemblies . . . by pointing to the greatest and oldest church, a church known to all men, which was founded and established at Rome by the most renowned Apostles Peter and Paul . . . . For it is a matter of necessity that with this Church, on account of its preeminent authority, every Church should agree, that is, the faithful everywhere, inasmuch as in her the apostolic tradition has been preserved continuously by those who are everywhere.[8]

---

6   *1 Clement*, 44.1–2.
7   Ignatius of Antioch, *Epistle to the Magnesians*, 14.
8   Irenaeus of Lyons, *Against Heresies*, 3.3.2.

## Did the Church only become hierarchical after Constantine?

Independent Evangelicals imagine that the church only became hierarchical after it was "infected" by the emperor Constantine's conversion in 315. At that time, they argue, the monarchical model came across from the court of the emperor and the church moved from being independent, local and congregational to being a centralized, hierarchical arm of the Roman Empire. Again, this theory has no relation to reality.

As we have seen, the idea of a monarchical papacy was there from the beginning, in Jesus' identity as the great scion of David the King with Peter as his steward. The steward, like the king he served, was to be the servant and shepherd of all, but he was also meant to rule through the charism of individual leadership. This form of governance was hierarchical from the beginning, for it is grounded in Jesus' own concept of the Kingdom of God. A kingdom is hierarchical through and through, and the church, as Christ's kingdom, is hierarchical from its foundations. Furthermore, the leadership of the Jewish church (on which the Christian church was modeled) was also hierarchical, with its orders of rabbis, priests and elders.

Obedience to the bishop as the head of the church was crucial. So Ignatius of Antioch writes to the Christians at Smyrna and condemns individualistic congregationalism in terms that are clearly hierarchical:

> All of you follow the bishop as Jesus Christ followed the Father, and the presbytery as the Apostles; respect the deacons as ordained by God. Let no one do anything that pertains to the church apart from the bishop. Let that be considered a valid Eucharist which is under the bishop or one who he has delegated . . . . It is not permitted to baptize or hold a love feast independently of the bishop.

The hierarchical nature of the church is confirmed and sealed through the apostolic succession. Church leaders are appointed by the successors of the apostles, and there is a clear chain of command which validates a church and its ministry. So Irenaeus writes,

> It is our duty to obey those presbyters who are in the Church who have their succession from the Apostles. . . . The others who stand apart from the primitive succession and assemble in any place whatever we ought to regard with suspicion either as heretics and

unsound in doctrine or as schismatics . . . all have fallen away from the truth.[9]

Throughout the New Testament and the writings of the Apostolic Fathers, the Church is portrayed as centralized, hierarchical and universal. The need for unity is stressed. Heresy and schism are anathema. Unity is guaranteed by allegiance to the clear hierarchical chain of command: God sent his Son Jesus. Jesus sent the Apostles. The Apostles appointed their successors. The Bishops are in charge. So Clement of Rome writes,

> The Apostles received the gospel for us from the Lord Jesus Christ: Jesus the Christ was sent from God. Thus, Christ is from God, and the Apostles from Christ. In both cases the process was orderly and derived from the will of God.[10]

## *Was Leo the Great the First Pope?*

The term "pope" is from the Greek word "*pappas*," which means "Father." In the first three centuries it was used of any bishop, and eventually the term was used for the Bishop of Alexandria, and finally by the sixth century it was used exclusively for the Bishop of Rome. Therefore, it is an open question who was the first "pope" as such.

The critics of the Catholic Church aren't really worried about when the term "pope" was first used. What they mean when they say that Leo the Great (440–461) was the first pope is that this is when the papacy began to assume worldly power. This is, therefore, simply a problem in definition of terms. By "pope," the Evangelical means what I thought of as "pope" after my Evangelical childhood. By "pope" they mean "corrupt earthly ruler." In that respect, Leo the Great might be termed the "first pope" because he was the one (in the face of the disintegrating Roman Empire) who stepped up and got involved in temporal power without apology.

However, to see the pope as merely a temporal ruler and then disapprove is to be too simplistic. Catholics understand the pope's power to be spiritual.

---

9 Irenaeus of Lyons, *Against Heresies*, 4.26.2.

10 *1 Clement*, 42.

While certain popes did assume temporal power, they often did so reluctantly, and did not always wield that power in a corrupt way. Whether popes should have assumed worldly wealth and power is arguable, but at the heart of their ministry, like the Lord they served, they should have known that their kingdom was not of this world. Their rule was to be hierarchical and monarchical in the sense that they were servants of the King of Kings and Lord of Lords. It was not first and foremost to be hierarchical and monarchical in the worldly sense.

The Protestant idea that the papacy was a fifth century invention relies on a false understanding of the papacy itself. After the establishment of the church at Constantine's conversion, the church hierarchy did indeed become more influential in the kingdoms of this world, but that is not the essence of the papacy. The essence of the papacy lies in Jesus' ordination of Peter as his royal steward, and his commission to assume the role of Good Shepherd in Christ's absence. The idea that Leo the Great was the first "pope" is therefore a red herring based on a misunderstanding of the pope's true role.

## *The Early Church Today*

From the Reformation onward, Protestant Christians have fallen into the trap of Restorationism. This is the idea that the existing church has become corrupt and departed from the true gospel and that a new church that is faithful to the New Testament can be created. These sincere Christians then attempt to "restore" the church by creating a new church. The problem is that each new group of Restorationists invariably creates a church of their own liking, determined by their contemporary cultural assumptions. They then imagine that the early church was like the one they have invented.

All of the historical documents show that, in essence, the closest thing we have today to the early church is actually the Catholic Church. In these main points, the Catholic Church is today what she has always been. Her leadership is unapologetically monarchical and hierarchical. Her teaching authority is centralized and universal, and the pope is what he has always been, the universal pastor of Christ's Church, the steward of Christ's kingdom and the Rock on which Christ builds his Church.

An Answer *Not* An Argument / Fr. Dwight Longenecker

# *The First Christians*

## HOW DO WE KNOW THE GOSPELS ARE HISTORICAL?

It is easy to exchange convinced assertions: "The gospels are 100% God's holy Word and every bit is historically accurate!" or "The gospels are fairy tales!" However, there is a discipline called "Biblical scholarship" in which scholars do some very interesting work determining just which parts of the gospels they think are reliable and which they think are not. Their conclusions are, of course, debated. That's what scholars do. Their work is fascinating, and it is worth taking some time to look at just a smidgen of their work and their methodology.

Bible scholars are most interested in trying to determine whether the original gospels record eyewitness accounts, and whether those original versions have been transmitted accurately. To do this scholars consider several factors. 1) authorship and date of composition, 2) intention and genre, 3) gospel sources and oral tradition, 4) textual criticism, and 5) historical authenticity of specific sayings and narrative events.

One of the difficult aspects for modern people to understand is just what kind of document the gospels are. Everyone can admit that they are not written as purely historical documents, but neither are they simply fabulous fables, myths or fairy tales. In continuity with the Old Testament and consistent with their Jewish origins, we have documents which are presented as history and have plenty of historically verifiable details, but which also have supernatural and otherworldly elements to them.

One of the ways to figure out just how the gospels writers deal with history is to consider the genre of literature they represent. New Testament scholar Graham Stanton writes, "the gospels are now widely considered to be a sub-set of the broad ancient literary genre of biographies." [1] It is also recognized that there are elements in the gospels that have a mythological character. So the gospels were written not strictly as objective biography, but with a theological intention. This is clear from reading the gospels themselves. The author of John's gospel writes, "These things are written that you might know that Jesus is the Christ, the Son of the Living God" (John 20:31). And New Testament scholar Erasmo Leiva-Merikakis writes that

> we must conclude, then, that the genre of the Gospel is not that of pure 'history'; but neither is it that of myth, fairy tale, or legend. In fact, 'gospel' constitutes a genre all its own, a surprising novelty in the literature of the ancient world.[2]

Historians therefore allow for the fact that these are essentially historical documents with what they call "mythological" elements woven into them. Whether the miracles or the "mythological elements" happened as the gospels report is open to debate. Believers accept the possibility of the miraculous. Non-believers do not. In each case the bias will affect the conclusion, but it must be said that one who believes miracles are possible is immediately more open-minded than one who has decided they are impossible. The believer is therefore open to more possibilities than the non-believer who entirely rules out miracles.

What many people miss, because of a secular or a scientific bias (or both), is that this sort of story is common to humanity everywhere. The supernatural or "mythological" is woven into the lives and stories of many individuals, families and cultures. Whether it is a near-death experience or a paranormal experience of some kind, or simply a more ordinary faith experience, people re-tell the remarkable things which have happened to them in ordinary life.

---

1   Graham Stanton, *Jesus and Gospel* (Cambridge University Press, 2004), 192.

2   Erasmo Leiva-Merikakis, *Meditations on the Gospel According to Saint Matthew*, Fire of Mercy, Heart of the Word 2 (San Francisco: Ignatius Press, 2004), 44.

Aunt Sally tells how she was healed at the summer camp revival meeting by Jesus Christ himself or Cousin Jimmy tells how he was miraculously preserved from falling headlong into a pot of acid by his guardian angel.

One does not have to accept the miraculous element of the story to acknowledge that Cousin Jimmy really did almost fall into a pot of acid, and that two workmates saw it happen at Florsheim Fertilizer Plant in Boondock, Missouri on January 27 at 3:00 in the afternoon. One does not have to accept that Aunt Sally was miraculously healed by Jesus to accept that she really did go to the revival meeting led by Pastor Billy Bob at the Hosanna Camp Meeting in Houndstooth, North Carolina on August third and that she went in feeling sick and came out feeling better. In other words, it is reasonable to attempt to sift out what is verifiable and provable from a reported story which, by its nature, is subjective and perceived as supernatural and therefore not verifiable with ordinary means of enquiry.

This is what scholars quite sensibly do when confronted with the gospel accounts. There are scholarly industries in themselves on the questions of authorship and date, sources and genre, but this chapter is concerned with the various tools used to help determine whether particular sayings or events from the recorded gospel accounts are authentic. There are several different scholarly means used to analyze the text.

The first tool the scholars us is called "criterion of dissimilarity." This says if something Jesus did or said clashed with the Jewish religion of his day (and therefore the religion of the first Christians), then it is more likely to be authentic. There are many examples of this. Indeed the whole gospel story can be seen as subversive to the existing Jewish religion. However, some specific examples would be Jesus talking alone to the woman at the well in Samaria, or the story of the Good Samaritan, or Jesus and his disciples breaking the Sabbath rules, or Jesus sharing the hospitality of sinners or standing the Ten Commandments on their head with his Sermon on the Mount.

The "criterion of embarrassment" says that if a saying or event was embarrassing to the memory of Jesus or the apostles it is more likely to be authentic. So Jesus losing his temper, clearing out the temple or calling a woman a "dog" are all examples. The apostles being proud, vain and doubting is another. So the story of Jesus being baptized by John would be authentic because it shows Jesus to be subordinate to John. Other examples are the supposed illegitimacy of Jesus' birth and the most obvious—his execution as a criminal.

The "criterion of multiple attestation" says that when two or more independent sources present similar or consistent accounts, it is more likely that the accounts are accurate reports of events or that they are reporting a tradition which pre-dates the sources themselves. This is often used to note that the four gospels attest to most of the same events. Paul's epistles often attest to these events as well, as do the writings of the early church, and to a limited degree, so do non-Christian ancient writings.

The "criterion of cultural and historical congruency" says that a source is less credible if the account contradicts known historical facts, or if it conflicts with cultural practices common in the period in question. Conversely, if the account matches up with the other known facts, it is more likely to be authentic. So the gospel stories are evaluated to see if they match with the known historical facts, the geography, archeological findings, cultural customs and details etc.

It should be noted that the results of these methods of textual analysis are not always unanimously in favor of the historicity of the gospels. However, the results are significantly satisfactory for professional historians and Biblical scholars working together to show that the gospels are, for the most part, historically reliable documents. Some scholars say that the historical parts have had mythological elements added to them through exaggeration or fabrication at a much later date.

One of the aspects of this analysis most often overlooked is the cross-referencing between the epistles of St. Paul and the gospels. Scholars are virtually unanimous in recognizing most of the epistles of St. Paul as having been written before his death in the Neronian persecutions in the year 65. The Book of Acts, while not authored by an eyewitness of Jesus' ministry, shows that the author knew the other apostles and indeed went to them for instruction and validation of his own ministry. Most importantly, the epistles are not written as gospels with the intention to glorify Jesus and make converts. They are letters to the early Christian communities scattered around the Roman Empire. They are therefore very accurate reflections of the people in those early communities and are accurate records of the beliefs of those early communities.

In his epistles, Paul quotes early Christian creeds that obviously predate his own writing. Scholars believe that these creeds date to within a few years of Jesus' death and developed in the early Christian communities. These texts are therefore an important and unique source for the study of early Christianity. 1 Corinthians 15:3–4, for example, reads: "For what I received I passed on to you as of first importance: that Christ died for our sins according to the Scriptures, that he was buried, that he was raised on the third day according to the Scriptures." The language formulations are different from Paul's own, indicating that he is quoting a mini-creed even earlier than his own writings, which were all written before A.D. 65. The antiquity of the creed has been located by many Biblical scholars to less than a decade after Jesus' death, originating from the Jerusalem apostolic community.

Concerning this creed, New Testament scholar Hans von Campenhausen said, "This account meets all the demands of historical reliability that could possibly be made of such a text;"[3] and A. M. Hunter wrote, "The passage therefore preserves uniquely early and verifiable testimony. It meets every reasonable demand of historical reliability."[4]

This is just one of about half a dozen such early creeds embedded in the writings of Paul. Here are some others: 1 John 4:2: "This is how you can recognize the Spirit of God: Every spirit that acknowledges that Jesus Christ has come in the flesh is from God," "regarding his Son, who as to his human nature was a descendant of David, and who through the spirit of holiness was declared with power to be the Son of God by his resurrection from the dead: Jesus Christ our Lord," and 1 Timothy 3:16: "He appeared in a body, was vindicated by the Spirit, was seen by angels, was preached among the nations, was believed on in the world, was taken up in glory."

What does it matter? What these early Christian creeds show is that the so-called mythological elements of the gospels (angels, resurrection, ascension into heaven, Son of God) were not much-later additions and accretions to the tradition, but were part of the beliefs about Jesus from the very earliest days.

---

3   "The Events of Easter and the Empty Tomb," in *Tradition and Life in the Church*, by Hans von Campenhausen (Philadelphia: Fortress Press, 1968), 44.

4   As quoted by Gary R. Habermas, *The Historical Jesus: Ancient Evidence for the Life of Christ* (College Press, 1996), 156.

## A CATHOLIC DATING SERVICE

That would be dating the New Testament—not dating an eligible young man or woman. While going on a date is important, the dating of the New Testament is more important—and here's why:

The closer the New Testament documents are to the historical events of the life of Jesus Christ, the more they can be trusted as being historically accurate.

If the New Testament documents are not to be trusted for their historicity, then the moral and doctrinal teachings found there are also debatable.

If the stories of the New Testament are fanciful constructions by Christians of a later date, then they can be dismissed as pious frauds. Likewise, the moral and doctrinal teaching can be dismissed as not really from Jesus himself.

From the rise of Biblical criticism in the late nineteenth and early twentieth century, modernist Protestant scholars like Friedrich Schleiermacher disputed the traditional early date of the New Testament documents. Those scholars likewise denied authentic apostolic authorship and dissected the texts using form criticism, linguistic criticism and historical criticism. Their critical method—rooted in rationalistic assumptions—soon jumped from the German theological schools to Anglicanism and Catholicism. The modern critical method seemed to bring the hard-edged tools of scholarship and a scientific method to the art of understanding Scripture.

The results were mixed. On the one hand, we now know far more about the intricacies of the Biblical texts, the historical background of the New Testament, and the complexion and intellectual world of the early church. On the other hand, the rationalistic foundations for modernist Biblical criticism have caused the supernatural elements of the New Testament to be sidelined, ignored, seen as later interpolations, or simply explained away.

As the critics did their work, a new generation of scholars succeeded them and continued to dismantle the New Testament—doubting more and more of the historical accounts of the gospels—until German theologian Rudolph Bultmann would famously assert not only that there was very little we could know about the historical Jesus, but that it didn't matter. Existential belief in Jesus was all that mattered, and not historical facts about Jesus.

## *Matter Matters*

Were you taught in Sunday School that history was "His Story"? Historicism is the heresy that denies such an idea. Historicism sees history as simply an accident of random events, rather than an overarching "meta narrative." Historicism is an outgrowth of atheism, for if there is no master storyteller, there can be no master story. For the modernist, as for the atheist, history doesn't matter, just as matter doesn't matter.

The doctrine of the incarnation, however, forces us to admit that matter matters. If God took human flesh in human history, then not only does human flesh matter, but history matters. The facts of the gospels cannot be dispensed with as meaningless or futile, leaving one with existential faith alone. Without the facts of the life of Christ, there is nothing in which faith can be rooted. St. Paul was blunt about this when he wrote, "If the resurrection did not happen our faith is in vain" (1 Cor. 15:14).

They say "The devil is in the details," but the divine is also in the details. If history matters, then facts matter and if facts matter, then details matter. It is therefore important whether Mark wrote Mark's gospel or not. It's important if Peter went to Rome or not. It's important to know if Paul really did write to the Christians in Corinth or not. Furthermore, modernist Biblical critics know that the details are important; otherwise they would not trouble themselves to dissect, dispute and deny them.

## *The Destruction of the Temple*

To date the New Testament accurately, one has to get involved in some clever detective work—piecing together a piece of the puzzle here and deducing how another missing piece might fit there. To do this, one of the first details any student of the gospel learns is the importance of the date A.D. 70. In the year 70, the Roman armies, finally wearied of a Jewish rebellion, besieged Jerusalem. After starving or slaughtering the inhabitants, they destroyed Jerusalem utterly and dispersed the survivors.

In the thirteenth chapter of Mark's gospel, Jesus clearly predicts the destruction of Jerusalem (Mark 13:1–2):

As Jesus was leaving the temple, one of his disciples said to him,

"Look, Teacher! What massive stones! What magnificent buildings!" But Jesus replied, "Do you see all these great buildings? Not one stone here will be left on another; every one will be thrown down."

With their rationalist presuppositions firmly in place, modern Biblical critics concluded that the entire New Testament could not have been composed before the year A.D. 70. The reasoning went like this: "Mark's gospel is the earliest gospel. Jesus predicted the destruction of Jerusalem. We know that people can't foretell the future. Therefore this must have been written after the event and made to sound like a prophecy." This one conclusion—based on the assumption that seeing the future is impossible—is the basis for the continuing idea that the New Testament is a late-invented document.

Once this "fact" was in place, every other piece of evidence relating to the dating of the gospels had to conform to this single conclusion. So if evidence was found that a particular gospel was written earlier than A.D. 70, it could not be so, because everyone "knew" that it all had to be written after A.D. 70. The authorship of the gospels therefore also had to be in question. If most of the apostles died before A.D. 70, the argument goes, then it was impossible for them to have been the authors of the gospels.

The entire edifice of New Testament scholarship therefore relies on this one iffy conclusion about the destruction of the temple in A.D. 70. The main problem with this conclusion is that it displays a remarkable ignorance about how prophecy actually works. A prophecy is not necessarily a supernatural event like some pagan soothsayer trying to read a crystal ball. Jesus' prophecy that Jerusalem would be destroyed may have been a supernatural vision of the future, but it could just as feasibly been a common sense realization of what would happen, knowing how the Romans treated rebels and knowing how inclined the Jews were to rebellion. It is not necessarily a supernatural gift to see how things are going and predict what will happen if they don't change.

## *The Deaths of Peter and Paul*

Jesus' prophecy of the destruction of Jerusalem is therefore not a reliable fixed point for determining the date of the New Testament. There is, however, an earlier reliable date: A.D. 65. We know this is the year St. Peter and St. Paul were killed in Rome during the persecution of the Emperor Nero. Therefore,

Paul's epistles and the first epistle of Peter were all written before A.D. 65.

We can also piece together the evidence to determine that other books of the New Testament also date from before the deaths of Peter and Paul in A.D. 65. The Acts of the Apostles was written by St. Luke—Paul's companion and the author of the gospel of Luke. In the Acts of the Apostles Peter and Paul are both still living. If Peter and Paul had died by the time Luke completed Acts of the Apostles, we can be sure he would have mentioned their deaths—especially since both were martyred.

Luke would have mentioned their martyrdom for three reasons: First, he told the story of Stephen's martyrdom. Secondly, he also related the death of the apostle James. Thirdly, the death of the martyrs was an important feature for the early Christians. They used it as a teaching point. John does just this in his mention of the death of Peter in his gospel.

Because the deaths of Peter and Paul are not mentioned in the Acts of the Apostles, we can be confident that it was written before A.D. 65. Furthermore, Luke makes it clear in the Acts of the Apostles that his gospel was the first volume he had written. Luke says in his opening words, "In my former book, Theophilus, I wrote about all that Jesus began to do and to teach until the day he was taken up to heaven, after giving instructions through the Holy Spirit to the apostles he had chosen" (Acts 1:1). If the Acts of the Apostles was written before A.D. 65, Luke's gospel must have been even earlier.

Many scholars believe the Gospel of Luke used the Gospels of Mark and Matthew as source material. If so, then the other two synoptic gospels are even earlier than Luke—which we've seen must be dated before A.D. 65. The fact that Mark and Matthew also do not record the deaths of the apostles points to the conclusion that their deaths had not yet taken place.

## *The Sons of Thunder*

This theory can be corroborated by an interesting detail about St. James. The snippet of evidence appears in the work of Justin Martyr. Justin was one of the early Christian writers called the Apostolic Fathers. He lived from A.D. 100–160, just about one hundred years after the death of Jesus. A convert to the church, Justin Martyr wrote various works defending the Christian faith. One of the details he recorded is this:

> It is said that he [Jesus] changed the name of one of the apostles to Peter; and it is written in his [Peter's] memoirs that he changed the names of others, two brothers, the sons of Zebedee, to Boanerges, which means "sons of thunder"....

What are Peter's "memoirs"? We know it isn't the *Gospel of Peter*—which is a later apocryphal gospel that was written long after Justin Martyr died. The early tradition of the church (recorded by Papias at the end of the first century) was that John Mark was the companion, translator and scribe for Peter, and that Mark's gospel is based on the memories of Peter himself.

Therefore, in the absence of any other writings that might be Peter's memoirs, we can safely conclude that the "memoirs" to which Justin Martyr refers are Mark's gospel. What seals the deal is that Mark is the only one of the Evangelists who records that Jesus nicknamed James and John "Boanerges—Sons of Thunder" (Mk. 3:17).

## *Peter and Mark in Rome*

If Justin Martyr knew of Peter's "memoirs" (which recorded a detail only found in Mark), then we can be confident that Mark was the companion and secretary of Peter. Furthermore, we know that Mark was in Rome with Peter because in his first epistle, Peter sends greetings from "Babylon" (which was early Christian code for Rome) and includes greetings from Mark.

Another intriguing detail from Mark's gospel points to Rome. In the passion narrative Mark records the fact that Simon of Cyrene was "the father of Rufus and Alexander" (Mk. 15:21). Why would Mark record such a detail unless his readers knew who Rufus and Alexander were? The early traditions say Rufus and Alexander became missionaries, and when he is writing to the church at Rome, Paul greets a certain "Rufus and his mother" (Romans 16:13).

What happened to Rufus' brother Alexander? In 1941, an archeologist discovered first century tombs of Cyrenian Jews in the Kidron Valley near Jerusalem. One of the ossuaries had the Greek inscription: Alexander, son of Simon. A son of "Simon" named Alexander buried in a first century Cyrenian cemetery in Jerusalem? Just a coincidence? Maybe by the time Paul wrote to the Romans, Alexander had died and only Rufus and his mother were still living and had fled to Rome.

Scholars believe Paul's letter to the Romans was written about A.D. 56. If the Rufus mentioned by Paul is the same person mentioned by Mark as the son of Simon of Cyrene, then Mark's gospel was not a late, pseudonymous document, but was written by Peter's companion Mark before A.D. 55—just over twenty years after the crucifixion of Jesus.

## *The Divine is in the Details*

The evidence just discussed is not all of the same quality. The evidence for the date for the death of Peter and Paul is very strong, and the silence about their death in the Acts of the Apostles also points very powerfully to a date for the three synoptic gospels as prior to A.D. 65. The documentary evidence from Justin Martyr and Papias is somewhat weaker for various reasons, and the evidence about Rufus and Rome is mere conjecture.

However, when all the evidence is put together, all the pieces of the puzzle begin to fit. As they do, the old foundation of modernist criticism begins to crumble. There is no real reason to suppose that the destruction of Jerusalem is the important date from which other dates should be reckoned. It is much more reliable to link the date of the death of the apostles to the writings that are actually by them or about them.

Since St. Paul died in A.D. 65, we can place all the epistles attributed to him before that date. Scholars may quibble about whether certain passages in the epistles of Paul are authentic or not. The main point is that the vast majority of writings attributed to Paul are of an early date. The A.D. 65 date also, as we have seen, points to a date for the synoptic gospels of prior to A.D. 55. That really only leaves the writings of the apostle John to be somewhat later—and even they must have been completed by around the turn of the first century, the time of John's death.

There is a popular myth circulating that the books of the New Testament are filled with late-invented mythical interpolations. Scholars like to imagine that a long time elapsed in which Greek philosophical and mythical ideas infected the early Christian texts. The early dating of the New Testament helps to dispel this myth. This early dating upholds the truth that the gospels are the authentic and reliable witness to the life, death and resurrection of Jesus Christ, and that the epistles record the remarkably early interpretations of those events for the world's salvation.

# PAGANISM, PROPHECIES AND PROPAGANDA

Did you know that Catholic bishops are actually high priests of Dagon, the ancient pagan deity of the Philistines? You see, the miter the bishop wears is a replica of the costumes worn by the priests of Dagon. That's right, the priests of Dagon wore a headdress that looked like the head of a fish with an open mouth, and down their back they wore a long cape that looked like the skin of a big fish. When you look at a Catholic bishop sideways you can see the open-mouthed fish head and his cope looks just like that fish skin they wore! This proves that Catholicism is really just old-fashioned, devil-worshipping, paganism—right? Wrong.

The bishop's miter developed from the *camelaucum*; a form of crown worn in the imperial court in Byzantium. There are no pictures of a Catholic bishop wearing what we would recognize as a miter until the eleventh century and then it was a shorter, softer hat which only developed into its present form in the late middle ages—long after the worshippers of Dagon were dead and gone.

## *Three Forms of Anti-Catholicism*

The true history of the bishop's miter is found with a simple search on the Internet, but explain this piece of historical detail to an extreme Protestant who believes everything Catholic is simply warmed up paganism, and you will discover that he thinks you have been brainwashed. The information on the Internet was a page on the Catholic Encyclopedia!! He will consider you to be a naive dupe of a sinister regime, and the source of your information is part of a cover-up by the Catholic disinformation machine in the secret walled city of the Vatican.

A second Protestant friend may not be quite so extreme in his beliefs that Catholic = pagan. He eschews the wild-eyed fundamentalism of the Chick Tracts. Nevertheless, he shakes his head sadly and informs you that Catholic doctrine is not Scriptural. It is a mishmash of pagan philosophy and religious customs. He tells you how veneration of the Virgin Mary and prayers to the saints have their roots in pagan goddess worship and ancestor worship.

He'll tell you how the doctrines of purgatory and the sacraments have come from Gnosticism, how transubstantiation is pagan Aristotelianism, and how Catholic beliefs on heaven and hell and the afterlife are infected with the pagan philosophies of Neo-Platonism.

Finally, there is your secular friend, with his own brand of Catholic = pagan anti-Catholicism. He does not fear Catholicism because it is pagan. He dismisses it because it is pagan. Secularists use the theory to ridicule or dismiss Catholicism because it shows that "all religions are merely different versions of primitive superstition."

## Protestant Propaganda

The idea that the Catholic Church is the pagan antichrist has been around since the Protestant Revolution. If your sect had been persecuted by the Catholic Church, it was easy enough to see the corrupt Roman hierarchy in the ominous warnings from the Book of Revelation.

When you read this quote from Revelation 17:3–6, you couldn't help but think of the opulence of the Roman prelates and the cardinals in their robes of purple and scarlet.

> I saw a woman sitting on a scarlet beast that was covered with blasphemous names and had seven heads and ten horns. The woman was dressed in purple and scarlet, and was glittering with gold, precious stones and pearls. She held a golden cup in her hand, filled with abominable things and the filth of her adulteries. The name written on her forehead was a mystery: BABYLON THE GREAT, THE MOTHER OF PROSTITUTES, AND OF THE ABOMINATIONS OF THE EARTH. I saw that the woman was drunk with the blood of God's holy people, the blood of those who bore testimony to Jesus.

Then when you read that the "seven heads" were the seven hills on which the harlot sat, and you knew that Rome was the city of seven hills, it would seem obvious: the Roman Catholic Church was that great whore.

It was only a short hop from there to connect all manner of Catholic beliefs and practices to the ancient pagan religions. With only a little bit of imagination (and inspiration from the Holy Spirit, of course) you soon came to see that Christmas and Easter were taken over from the pagan Spring and

Winter celebrations, that the "worship" of the Blessed Virgin Mary was derived from the ancient cult of Diana of the Ephesians, that the Eucharist was taken from Egyptian fertility rites, Baptism and the idea of the "sacraments" were lifted from Mithraism and yes, the bishop's miter was really part of the secret worship of Dagon, the fish god of the Philistines.

The list could go on and on. In fact, it is only limited by the imagination of those who wish to discover pagan antecedents to Catholicism. It's simple. Look hard enough and you will find what you seek. Begin with your theory and then find the "facts" to support it. All of these "historical" theories can be easily refuted with a bit of research and explanation. Instead of tackling the different theories, though, I would like to unlock the thinking behind the "Catholicism is rehashed paganism" fable and show how best to counter it.

## *Pervasive Propaganda*

It is easy to think that the "Catholicism is rehashed paganism" notion is only put out by extremist Protestants like Jack Chick in his lurid "Christian comics," but the assumption that ancient paganism was adopted into Catholicism is standard within every level of Protestantism. It may not be as extreme and wacky as the Chick tracts or the idea that the bishop's miter is a carryover from the worship of Dagon, but most Protestants believe that at least some Catholic customs are pagan in origin.

Furthermore, the idea that Catholicism is merely paganism reborn is very prevalent among secular critics of the Church. Protestants use the theory to dismiss Catholicism with horror because they think all paganism is of the devil.

The way to counter both arguments is to admit that the ancient pagan religions influenced the development of Christianity, but to show why this is natural and harmless, and why it means neither that Catholicism is devil worship nor that it is simply primitive superstition.

## *The Missing Link*

The first thing to say to a Protestant who blames Catholicism for "being pagan" is to admit that elements of the ancient pagan culture did influence the development of Christianity.

However, he should do his homework and find out for sure. Just because two things happened at the same time does not demand a link between them, and it certainly does not demand a causal link. So, for example, the decline of the number of Catholic priests and nuns in the United States coincided with the popularity of Elvis Presley and the decline in popularity of Bing Crosby. This does not mean that the two phenomena were linked (even though Bing Crosby played the part of a Catholic priest) and it certainly doesn't mean that the popularity of Elvis Presley caused the decline in the number of priests.

Likewise, to see the similarity between two things and their coinciding does not require that they be linked in any way, and it certainly does not prove a causal link between the two. Even if a cultural link can be proved, there also must be proof of which way the causal link flows. Does the existence of a Winter solstice celebration in both Christianity and Roman paganism demand that one caused the other? If so, which one influenced the other? It used to be a commonplace belief that the Christians borrowed the pagan Winter Saturnalia for Christmas. It now seems that the reverse is true. The pagans instituted the Saturnalia as competition for the increasingly popular feast of the Nativity of Christ.

## *We're All Pagan*

The second point to make to the Protestant who blames Catholicism for being pagan is to point out that the things he believes have links with paganism too. He may think that veneration of the Blessed Virgin Mary is "pagan," but the doctrines he holds to could be seen to have pagan antecedents as well. He believes in the Virgin Birth and the incarnation, but pagan religions are full of stories of Virgins giving birth to god-men. Does he believe in the Resurrection? Does he celebrate it at Easter? How does he fit that in with the common pagan myths of the dying and rising god who was worshipped annually at the springtime of the year? Does he believe in the inspiration of the Holy Spirit? The Ascension? Baptism? The Eucharist? All of these beliefs and practices have their parallels in paganism. He can't blame Catholics for being pagan in some beliefs and practices while he himself happily endorses beliefs that might also have their origins in paganism.

This is the crux of the argument. Your Protestant friend should realize that there are links between paganism and Christianity and that this is natural because the church was born in a particular culture which was bound to influence it, and that there is nothing wrong with this happening. From the very beginning this was considered to be good missionary method: find what connects with the Christian story in the culture you are preaching to, make the connection, build on that and then use it to share the Christian gospel through images with which they are familiar.

Finally, remind your Protestant friend that this is precisely what we see taking place in the New Testament. So in Acts, St. Paul preaches in Athens and sees in the temple an altar to an "unknown god." He picks up on this and uses the concept to preach the gospel. Sometimes the "Catholic is paganism reborn" argument moves from practices like praying for the dead or the veneration of saints to accusations that Catholic theology is infected with pagan philosophies like Gnosticism or Platonism.

At this point remind your Protestant friend that St. John used the existing Greek philosophical concept of the *logos* (the Word) to articulate the doctrine of the pre-existing Son of God and the incarnation of the Son of Man. Remind them that St. Paul uses the concept of "the mystery of godliness" throughout his writings, and in doing so is connecting with his pagan audience's awareness of the mystery religions. Likewise, the epistle to the Hebrews, with its talk of an "earthly temple" (an image of the "heavenly temple") is steeped in a Platonic metaphysical understanding.

## *So What?*

The secular critic of the Catholic faith also argues that Catholicism is simply a rehash of paganism. His argument comes from the humanistic understanding of the history of religion. It goes like this:

"All religions developed when human beings were primitive. They looked at the sun, moon and stars and were awed by them. They gave them personalities and made up stories about them. These became the gods and goddesses of ancient myths. Then they thought there should be just one god. This god became the God of the Hebrews and then then Christianity emerged from the Hebrew religion, but took on lots of the traits of paganism too, and that is why it was so successful."

Having equated Christianity with all the other primitive superstitions, they can smugly dismiss its claims. The final answer to both the secularist and the fundamentalist is the same. It requires an explanation of just how and why there are connections and links between Christianity and other religions.

## *Hints and Glimpses*

When someone dismissed Christianity because of its links with pagan religions, C. S. Lewis observed that it would trouble him more if Christianity *didn't* have links with other religions. The fact is, you can find similarities and connecting points between Christianity and all the other religions both ancient and modern, and it is this fact which validates, rather than invalidates, Christianity.

Since the Christian faith (and more specifically the Catholic faith) connects in its beliefs and practices with other religions, it shows that Catholicism is deeply true. What we would be suspicious of is a religion that was totally isolated and cut off from every other world religion. Such a religion would have to be made up. Since there are links and connections with other religions, they shed light on the Catholic faith and illuminate the depths of Catholicism.

The Catholic understanding is that all the other religions—ancient pagan religions and modern religions—all point to the fullness of truth which is found in the Catholic faith. The pagan religions in their own way point to and prophesy the coming of Christ. This was the view of the Church Fathers. They looked to the pagan myths and saw glimpses and hints of the Christ who was to come. They saw the ancient religious systems and practices and devotions and saw in them all a kind of prophecy and pointer to the Christ who was to come.

Every aspect of the ancient world was thought by the Fathers to be a pointer to Christ. The pagan philosophers also pointed to Christ. In their images, their language and their systems of thought, they were hinting at what was to come. So the Fathers of the Church loved to pull out quotes from the ancient philosophers which hinted at the fullness of revelation that would come in Christ, such as this one from the Roman poet Virgil, writing around 40 BC:

Now the virgin is returning . . .

A new human race is descending from the heights of heaven . . .

The birth of a child, with whom

the iron age of humanity will

end and the golden age begin.[1]

Catholicism is not the practice of paganism, but it is the fulfillment of the hints and glimpses that are given in every ancient religion, philosophy and prophecy. Truth, wherever it appears, is Catholic truth, and once we see the relationship between other religions and philosophies and the Catholic faith, the sooner we will see their beautiful fulfillment in the one true faith.

---

1   Virgil, *Eclogues* IV. 5–10.

# THE PROBLEMS WITH PRIMITIVISM

As a boy, I attended a church that was founded in 1962. It grew from a group of Christians meeting together in their homes for Bible study. They were disenchanted with the liberal drift of their mainstream Protestant denominations and decided to go back to basics. They did not believe they were doing anything new. Instead they were returning to the simple principles of the early church.

From their reading of the New Testament, they concluded that the first Christians met in homes to sing hymns, study the Bible and pray together. Eventually they wrote a constitution, bought land and built a church building and school. They did not regard this as anything more than a natural outgrowth of their first, simple communal meetings in their homes.

The idea that a new church or denomination is really a return to the earliest days of Christianity is called Restorationism or Christian Primitivism, and it is written into the genetic code of most Protestant churchgoers as a basic assumption.

Primitivism may be part of the foundation of Protestantism, but it is a foundation that is fatally flawed. Before we examine the problems of Primitivism, though, it is worth looking at its history.

## *Let's Start at the Very Beginning*

The urge to shed accumulated "traditions of men" and return to the pristine gospel as taught by Jesus to the apostles is nothing new. The first Christians to fall into this trap may have been the Montanists in the mid-second century. Like modern-day Pentecostals, the Montanists emphasized the work of the Holy Spirit and prophecy. Their opposition to the organized church and "loyalty" to the Holy Spirit suggests a Restorationist agenda.

Other ancient heretical groups had Primitivist tendencies, but the first separatist group to be clearly driven by Restorationist zeal, were the Paulicians. They were founded in the mid-600s by an Armenian named Constantine, who claimed to be restoring the pure Christianity of St. Paul. The Paulicians were Adoptionists (believing that Jesus became the Son of God at his baptism). Influenced by Manichaeism, they rejected infant Baptism, the clergy, monasticism, the doctrine of the real presence, and all iconography.

In Bulgaria three hundred years later, a new shoot sprang out of the Paulician sect. The Bogomils (meaning Dear Ones of God) grew in reaction to the corrupt established church of their time. They met in their own homes, rejected the priesthood, rejected the doctrine of the real presence and believed that all should be taught by the simple-minded. They also rejected monasticism and did not accept marriage as a sacrament. Like the Paulicians, the Bogomils were dualists—believing in equal good and evil forces in the world.

Henry the Monk and Waldes (from whom the Waldensians are descended) were wandering preachers in the twelfth century who lived simple lives and preached against the corruption of the church. They gathered groups of disciples around them, while at the same time the Cathars carried on the dualistic and heretical teaching of the Bogomils. All these pre-Reformation groups, Restorationist in their ideals, were the precursors of the Protestant Reformation.

## *Anti-Tradition Tradition*

Restorationists might be opposed to human tradition, but by the sixteenth century they had developed their own venerable anti-establishment traditions. Often their reasons were sincere and urgent. Wherever the church is corrupt, complex and privileged, the urge for Restorationism is strong. People long for a simple, pristine and pure church of long ago. Simple Christians want the church to be for simple people. They read the gospel and see Christ ministering to the outcasts, the sick and the ordinary people and believe that is what the Church should be like. They are not wrong in their desire for simplicity and reform, so it is easy to see why Restorationist movements are so attractive and successful.

While Luther and Calvin initially wished to reform the established church, the more extreme Protestants were radical in their Restorationist zeal. The Hussites and the Anabaptists were the most radical, and it is the radical Restorationism of the Anabaptists which comes down to us today as the grand-daddy of all the subsequent Restorationist movements.

The Anabaptist line continues through the Quakers, Shakers and other sects to the Landmarkists, who claim a line of succession for Baptists right back to John the Baptist. The Calvinist and Wesleyan "Great Awakening" in the eighteenth century was radically Restorationist, followed by the similarly Restorationist "Second Great Awakening" in the United States. By now, though, the Restorationists were not only reacting against the Catholic Church, but against all the other historic Protestant denominations.

Through the nineteenth century in America, wave after wave of Restorationist churches sprang up, such as the Christadelphians, Christian Conventions, Seventh Day Adventists, Latter Day Saints, and Jehovah's Witnesses. At the same time a strong Restorationist movement (the Cambellites) fostered independent groups like the Churches of Christ, Disciples of Christ and Christian Church.

The tradition continues today with each new wave of Protestantism reacting not only against Catholicism and liberal Protestantism, but also against the previous generation of Restorationists. In the 1960s, my family attended an independent fundamental Bible Church. Then in the 1970s, the charismatics, with their house churches and local communities, picked up the Restorationist baton. The 1980s saw the growth of charismatic megachurches like John Wimber's Vineyard, and now a whole range of local community churches fly the Restorationist flag. For all their rejection of tradition, it seems the Restorationists follow their own well-established traditions.

## *The Problems with Primitivism*

Zipping through the history of Christian Primitivism helps us understand the problems with this admirable but flawed ideal. There are eight problems with Primitivism. When they are outlined, the fragile foundations of the whole movement tremble, and consequently the intellectual support for the whole edifice must fall.

Firstly, each Restorationist movement, although it seeks to return to the ancient, pristine and timeless church of the apostolic age, is actually devised and determined by a reaction to the circumstances of its own age and cultural necessities. So, for example, the peasant movement of the Bogomils came out of a church weighed down with corruption and aristocratic influence. The radical reformers in sixteenth century Europe and the New World were influenced by the utopianism, the rise of the nation-state, and the revolutionary spirit of their age. Similarly, the American Restorationist movement of the eighteenth and nineteenth centuries was determined more by the independent, anti-establishment mentality of the American frontier than by any real reference to the church of the apostolic age. Restorationists do not restore anything ancient. Their "restoration" is never more than a reflection of the circumstances and the assumptions of the age in which they live.

The second problem with Primitivism is that each Primitivist group clashes with the others. If Primitivism were a proper instinct, and each Primitivist group was simply returning to a beautiful, basic Bible religion, wouldn't they all agree? There are certainly similarities between many of the groups, but there are more disagreements than agreements. Which ones have really discovered what the primitive church was like? The dualistic Bogomils and Cathars or the apocalyptic Adventists and Millerites? Would it be the Christadelphians who deny the gifts of the Holy Spirit or the Charismatics who do not?

The third problem with Primitivism is its ignorance of what the Primitive Church was really like. The Primitivists assume that the early church met in people's homes and was congregational, not hierarchical, as well as being non-liturgical, Bible-based, and non-sacramental. All of these assumptions are simply not true, or if they were true in some places, they are not the whole truth.

The reason the Primitivists are ignorant of what the primitive Church was really like is because they are largely unaware of the writings of the Early Church fathers. They do not know that we have documents telling us just what the early Christians believed, how they worshipped, and how the Church was structured. While they are keen on restoring the primitive church, the Primitivists remain largely ignorant of the facts we do have on what the early church was really like. Therefore, their ecclesial creations are not reproductions of the primitive Christian church, but manifestations of their own pious imagination.

This ignorance about what the early church was really like might be put down to their belief in *Sola Scriptura*. The Christian Primitivist believes that his hymn-singing, Bible studying little home church is what is found in the Bible. Even that is unsupportable. While we do find examples of house churches in the New Testament (Rom. 16:5; 1Cor. 16:19; Col. 4:15), we also find the apostles meeting for worship regularly in the Temple, (Acts 2:46; 3:1; 5:42). St. Paul always went to worship first in the synagogue when he went to a new city in his missionary travels (Acts 14:1; 17:2). Furthermore, liturgical and Biblical experts like Louis Bouyer and Gregory Dix tell us that the early Christian worship was patterned after Jewish worship, which meant that it was liturgical in structure and sacramental in character. If they met in homes, it was only because the church was persecuted, not because there was any intrinsic merit in house churches.

We need only look at the Scriptures to see that the church was hierarchical, not democratic. While there is a Council of Jerusalem, it is a council of the Apostles and Elders of the Church. The simple, congregational, non-liturgical model of the Primitivists is based on their own highly selective reading of the New Testament, not on a thorough study of either the New Testament or the other documents of the age. Like all Protestants, the Primitivist is his own Pope. He not only interprets the Bible according to his own ideas; he interprets history according to his own assumptions, expectations and need.

## *Primitivism's Problem Principles*

These external problems with Primitivism reveal deep fractures in the edifice of Primitivism, but the fractures are there because of deeper fault lines that run through the foundations. The main problems with Primitivism are at ground level. Like all foundations, they lay hidden, but it is in examining the foundations that we see the deeper problems.

Christian Primitivism is based on the assumption that there is no such thing as an infallible church. For the Primitivist there cannot be an infallible church; otherwise, the church would not have strayed so radically from the truth. Because the church has (so obviously) departed from the truth, the argument goes, she cannot be infallible.

But this assumption is leaky, because the Primitivist's whole enterprise is an attempt to recover a church that was pristine and pure and (by inference) infallible. Either there was an ancient infallible church, in which case it has never failed because it cannot fail, or there was never an ancient infallible church, in which case, why bother to attempt a recovery of it?

The sixth problem is connected with the fifth. Primitivism is based on the assumption that the Catholic Church is not infallible, and that there is no such thing as an infallible church, but the Primitivist would have us believe that his "restored" church is infallible. It is true that he does not state this belief openly, yet he heartily believes it is so, for he has given his total allegiance to this church. But if his restored church is infallible, why did God allow six or ten or nineteen centuries to pass before establishing it? If, on the other hand, this restored church is not infallible, why should I (or anyone else for that matter) be expected to owe allegiance to it?

The seventh and eighth problems of Primitivism are the most blatant naked emperor of all. Firstly, assuming that the primitive church is the church of the first century (and this assumes that there is a cutoff point when the church ceases to be "primitive"—and who decides that?), how can anyone really know what the first century church was like? We have archeological evidence. We have Scriptural evidence. We have documentary evidence, but we cannot really get back into the skin of first century Christians in the Roman Empire. We can't really understand the culture, the assumptions and the worldview of former Jewish and Gentile Christians in the Roman Empire.

Even if we could come up with an accurate checklist of all the attributes of the primitive church, who would decide which of the attributes we wanted to re-create and which ones we would omit? Shall we have house churches but not women covering their heads in church? Shall we have simple Bible preaching, but not speaking in tongues and miraculous handkerchiefs? Shall we have sacraments but not slaves? Finally, why should it necessarily be a good thing to re-create the primitive church at all? We live in the twenty-first century, not the first century. Any attempt at recovery can never be anything more than an artificial reproduction—with the same relationship to primitive Christianity as Cinderella's castle at Disneyland has to a chateau in France.

## *The Alternative*

When faced with a church that is corrupt, complex, and seemingly out of touch, Christian Primitivism is an admirable ideal. Given the assumption that the Catholic Church cannot possibly be correct, to establish a simple, down to earth form of Christianity is laudable. If one is going to start a religion, it is a good thing to wish for that religion to be the ancient faith that comes to us from the Apostles.

Given that it is a laudable thing to want one's church to be connected with the Church of the first century, and accepting the arguments put forward here on the intrinsic flaws of Primitivism, one has therefore to ask if any link with the primitive church exists, and if it does, where one might find it.

Catholics have always believed that the primitive church never ceased to exist. It was established by Jesus Christ himself on the rock of Peter and his divinely inspired profession that Jesus was the Son of God. This church, as Christ promised, has withstood the test of time. She has been buffeted by corruption from within and persecuted by enemies from without. Nevertheless, the gates of hell have not prevailed against her.

The primitive church may have become more complex, but she did not cease to preach constantly the simple message of Jesus Christ and his saving work on the cross. The primitive church may have adapted and changed and grown throughout two thousand years of history, but she has not become something different. Her understanding of the apostolic deposit of faith may have developed and matured, but she did not alter that faith once delivered to the saints. Members of that primitive church may have stumbled and fallen; they may have sinned and caused scandal; they may have obscured the gospel and betrayed the gospel, but in every age there have always been saints who have remained radiantly faithful.

Catholics maintain today, as we have always done, that the primitive church is alive in the world as she has always been. Just as the simple pauper's tomb of the fisherman lies beneath the soaring dome of St. Peter's, so the primitive church lies at the heart of Catholicism.

At her head is the successor of Peter and at her feet is a world more in need of her message of forgiveness and love than ever before. It is a good thing to search for the primitive church, but why embark on an empty quest to create your own when the Catholic Church stands waiting—ever ancient and ever new?

# *Sacraments and Salvation*

## ONE SAVING ACTION

I married my wife Alison about twenty-five years ago. On that day we made a vow to remain married—for better, for worse, for richer, for poorer, until death should part us. That vow was a once and for all mutual promise. It was a step of faith. I accepted Alison and she accepted me. We loved each other, but realized that our love would have to grow over the years. Our marriage vow took place in one moment in time, but you could say it is present in every moment of our married life. We took a step of faith to marry one another, but we have to live within that faith day by day and moment by moment for our vows to be real.

If we do not perform the faithful actions of love within our marriage and family life, then that promise of love eventually dies. However, if we lived together without having made the vows, our life would not be the same as if we had married. A legal analyst might wish to study the purely formal aspect of our marriage, but that wouldn't be the marriage. Likewise, a psychologist or sociologist might like to study the day to day life of our relationship, but that wouldn't be the marriage either. The vows and the daily life go together. The vows we made help us live in love day by day and our daily life of love is the fulfilment of the vows. Separating our marriage vows from our marriage is impossible. Separating the two would be like trying to separate the light from the sun, the scent from the flower or the music from the violin from which it comes.

One of the biggest areas of confusion and misunderstanding between Catholics and other Christians is in the area of salvation. How is a person saved? How does a person get to heaven? Is it by their works or by their faith? One of the classic Protestant doctrines is that we are saved by faith alone. In the sixteenth century, Martin Luther and others felt their Catholic faith was legalistic and meaningless. It was just a set of rules and routine, formal prayers which meant nothing and which could never save a person. When Martin Luther read St. Paul's letter to the Romans he discovered for himself the wonderful Biblical doctrine that a person is saved by grace through faith—and not by any works they have done.

This was exciting and liberating news. No longer did people have to be good enough to please God by reciting endless liturgies, enduring grueling asceticism and achieving an impossible standard of goodness. God had saved them through the work of Jesus Christ and all they had to do was trust in him through faith to be saved. Because they had discovered salvation by grace through faith, some of them took the extreme position that a person is saved through faith alone. In their enthusiasm to embrace salvation by faith alone, and remembering how they felt helpless to do all the good works they thought were expected of them as Catholics, they couldn't help drawing the conclusion that the Catholic church taught that a person was saved by good works.

It must have seemed as if that was the teaching of the Catholic church at the time, and perhaps a lot of ordinary people felt that their salvation was won by endless prayer and good works. In fact, though, the Catholic Church has never taught that salvation is through good works. The idea that we can work our way into heaven is a heresy called Pelagianism, after a fourth century teacher named Pelagius. From that time, and down through the ages, the Catholic Church has repudiated such teaching. That doesn't mean the Catholic Church believes in salvation by faith alone, though. We believe salvation is through faith, but we believe faith consists of more than an individual's personal belief. For faith to be real, it has to include the person's whole life. Catholics agree that we are saved by grace alone, but not by faith alone.

An exciting new document was signed in 1998 by Lutherans and Catholics at the highest level. The *Joint Declaration on the Doctrine of Justification* included the statement,

By grace alone, in faith in Christ's saving work and not because of any merit on our part, we are accepted by God and receive the Holy Spirit, who renews our hearts while equipping and calling us to good works.[1]

The zeal of Catholics for salvation by God's grace alone is summed up in the words of one of the greatest saints of modern times. Thérèse of Lisieux wrote,

> In the evening of this life, I shall appear before you empty-handed, for I do not ask you, Lord, to count my works. All our justices have stains in your sight. So I want to be clad in your own justice and receive from your love the possession of yourself.[2]

One of the problems in this debate between the need for faith or works is that both sides have tended to pull out certain verses from the New Testament to use as proof texts. The Evangelicals use some verses from St. Paul's teaching that "a man is saved by faith, and not by any works of the law lest any man should boast" (Eph. 2:8–9). Catholics respond with verses from the epistle of James which say clearly that "faith without works is dead" (James 2:26). But this is a bit like two cowboys in a shootout—both of them pull out their six-guns and shoot from the hip. The problem is, they're arguing away, but neither is actually listening to the other, and the only person each convinces is himself.

Common sense tells us that faith and works are both important, and in practice, most Catholics and Protestants actually agree that both are necessary to some extent. I think the best way to confront this whole issue is to avoid simple proof texts on their own, and to steer around the strong language and emotional experiences of the Reformation times by turning back to the Bible as a whole. The Bible shows that faith and works are one. The first part of this chapter is going to be a Biblical exploration of what the Bible says about faith and works. The second part explains in more detail how Catholics see the two operating together. This is a huge issue to which shelves of theological libraries devote yards of space. I should say that I'm neither a Biblical scholar or a theologian. I write this as a parish priest in hopes that what I say might help others to think through this issue.

---

1 *Joint Declaration on the Doctrine of Justification*, 15.

2 Therese de Lisieux, *Story of a Soul: The Autobiography of St. Therese of Lisieux*, trans. John Clarke, 3rd edition (Lisieux: I C S Publications, 1996), 277.

## *Faith of our Fathers*

The place to begin is the Old Testament, but in the Old Testament, we don't actually hear too much about faith as such. When the word "faith" is used it usually means keeping one's word—keeping a solemn agreement between two parties. Where it is used in a religious context, faith for the Jewish person means keeping his part of the solemn covenant between God and his people. The way the Jewish person kept his side of the covenant was by obeying the law. It almost sounds like the Old Testament definition for faith is actually good works, because the basic meaning of "keeping faith" in the Old Testament means keeping the law, or obeying God's commandments.

However, there are one or two other hints in the Old Testament that "having faith" could mean something more. In 2 Chronicles 20:20, the good king Jehosophat calls on the people to "Have faith in the Lord your God and you will be upheld. Have faith in his prophets and you will have success." Then the prophet Habakkuk looks forward to the day when the Lord's messenger will come and bring the revelation of God. In that day, says the prophet, "the righteous will live by faith" (Hab 2:4). But in the context, the word "faith" also means "faithfulness," so Habakkuk is saying that the one who is loyal, or faithful, or who keeps his part of the bargain will be considered righteous.

All through the Old Testament the person who has faith is also faithful, or loyal. The person who has faith obeys the covenant and keeps his side of the bargain. But what does this mean in action? Are there any illustrations of faith in the Old Testament? What does the person of faith look like? What does he believe and what does he do to keep his side of the bargain with God? The New Testament Book of Hebrews helps us see the Old Testament through Christian eyes, and in Chapter 11 it speaks at great length about the faith of the Old Testament characters. Hebrews sees that they were faithful because they had faith in God. In other words, they were able to be loyal and obedient because they trusted in God's faithfulness. They were able to keep their end of the bargain because they knew God would keep his.

Hebrews 11 goes through a list of the Old Testament characters showing their faithfulness. It reads like an Old Testament Hall of Fame. First is Adam and Eve's son Abel. He makes a better sacrifice than Cain because he has faith in God. By faith Noah believed God and built an ark to save himself and his family from destruction. By faith Abraham left the city of his fathers and set out to a country that God promised to him. By faith Abraham was able to become a father even though he was past the age because he considered God to be faithful. By faith Abraham offered his son Isaac as a sacrifice—believing that God could even raise the dead.

The interesting thing to note in this list from Hebrews is that each one of the Old Testament characters is considered to have faith, but as a result of this faith they perform faith-full actions—actions that are full of faith. Abel offers a sacrifice, Noah builds an ark, Abraham sets out on pilgrimage, fathers a son and then offers him as a sacrifice. Hebrews says by faith they performed these obedient and faith-full actions. The list from the Old Testament goes on, and in each case, the Old Testament hero is able to perform acts of faith because he believes in God. So Hebrews 11 continues—Isaac blessed Jacob because he had faith. By faith Jacob blessed his sons, by faith Joseph prophesied the Exodus from Egypt. By faith Moses' parents hid him in the river. By faith Moses led the people of Israel and instituted the Passover meal. By faith he led them through the Red Sea, conquered Jericho and entered the Promised Land. The writer to the Hebrews goes on to list the heroes from the book of Judges and beyond. By faith they conquered kingdoms, administered justice, shut the mouths of lions, quenched the fury of the flames, became powerful in battle, and went through terrible persecutions.

The list recounting the Old Testament heroes is dynamic, full of action and excitement. Faith enabled all these heroes to perform actions that were courageous and faithful to God's commands. Those actions were not mindless and arbitrary acts of obedience. The actions themselves were meaningful. They taught the faithful ones lessons about themselves and God. They performed God's will in the world and they helped bring the faithful ones to a higher perfection. The great chapter on faith in Hebrews shows that personal faith and faith-full actions together helped bring the believer into a deeper relationship with God. Their faith was not simply belief in God's promises or a personal belief in certain truths about God. Instead their faith was inner belief lived out through their decisions and actions.

In the Old Testament, then, the righteous person lives by faith, and his faith or trust in God is always shown through his obedient faith-full actions. The Old Testament therefore doesn't say too much about faith as such, but when Jesus comes on the scene the Scriptures suddenly explode with references to faith. Time and again Jesus scolds his disciples because they do not have enough faith.

He says if they have only a little faith they could move mountains. It is by faith that people are healed, and it is through faith that his disciples will do great signs and wonders. In the Old Testament, faith was linked with faithful obedience to God's law, but now faith becomes a dynamic power source in the person's life. Suddenly Jesus' disciples will be able to do great things through faith.

Jesus doesn't say in whom or what they are to have faith. As Jews, his disciples would have put their faith in God alone—the ultimate faithful one; and for them having faith meant obeying God's commands. But in John 2:11 we read that the disciples put their faith in Jesus, and throughout the gospels we're told that people put their faith in Jesus himself. In other words, they transferred their faith in the law-giving God to the person of Jesus Christ. This is an astounding transition, because in putting their faith in Jesus they were recognizing him to be the faithful one. In other words, they were recognizing that their solemn agreement to be in a covenant relationship with God was fulfilled by being in a relationship with Jesus.

Then in John 14:12, Jesus says something even more stupendous. Just before he promises the Holy Spirit he says, "I tell you the truth, anyone who has faith in me will do what I have been doing. He will do even greater things than these because I am going to the Father." All through the gospels, Jesus fulfils the Old Testament and here he fulfils the incomplete Old Testament idea of faith. In the Old Testament, faith was the obedient response to believing in a God who was trustworthy and good. Now faith is linked to a real person in place and time—Jesus. Furthermore, faith now includes a personal relationship and it empowers the disciples to do what Jesus does.

In the next passage in John 14, Jesus speaks further about the person who has faith in him. He will receive the Holy Spirit, and he will also have a certain new responsibility. In verse 15 he says, 'If you love me you will obey what I command. And I will ask the Father and he will send another Counsellor to be with you forever—the Spirit of Truth." Jesus promises that he will live in them and they will live in him. The evidence of this is that they will obey his teachings and do what he has done. In verse 20, he says, "On that day you will realize that I am in my Father, and you are in me, and I am in you. Whoever has my commands and obeys them, he is the one who loves me." This is the final and most profound dimension to faith. In John's gospel, it becomes clear that having faith in Jesus means entering into a supernatural union with him. If you like, faith makes the person a part of Jesus—a member of his body. Through this faith they think his thoughts and do his actions in the world. Faith here is not simply belief that Jesus is the Son of God, it is a personal union with Him.

The fact that this passage is intertwined with his promise of the Holy Spirit shows us that the faith and the good works that flow from faith both have their ultimate origin from God the Holy Spirit. In other words, both faith in Jesus and the actions of Jesus which we do are initiated and carried out by the working of God within us. God gives us a little bit of his power in order to become unified with Jesus Christ and then do his works in the world. This gift of God's goodness, power and light is called Grace. Both Catholics and Evangelicals agree on this point—that we can neither have faith nor can we do faith-full good works without the gift of God's grace which empowers us.

A person may have faith, but what does this person of faith have to do? Must they still obey the Old Testament law? Well, in one passage Jesus tells the disciples that they must actually be more righteous than the Scribes and Pharisees—those respectable religious people who obeyed every detail of the law. What he meant by this was not so much that they had to obey the Old Testament law, but that their new kind of righteousness was to outstrip the Old Testament obedience. It was to be a fresh kind of goodness—as different to the old legalistic way as a color photo is to a black and white picture. Obeying Christ's commands is not just an action of pure obedience as it was in the Old Testament. Instead, obeying Christ's commands is the way to enter more fully into unity with him. As the apostle John says, "whoever keeps his word, in him true love for God is perfected. By this we may be sure that we are in him: he who says he abides in him ought to walk in the same way in which he walked" (1 Jn. 2:5–6). Therefore, obeying his commands in faith is the method by which Jesus' disciples will dwell in him, become like him, and be made perfect.

The Book of Hebrews always shows that the Old Testament heroes of faith did certain actions by faith. Likewise, in the gospels, Jesus the man of faith is always acting out that faith with his life, his teachings, his death and his resurrection. So faith which is not acted out in the world is not faith at all—it is only an idea. Faith which is just a personal inner religious experience is incomplete. So in Matthew 7:21, Jesus says, "Not everyone who says Lord, Lord will enter the kingdom of heaven, but only those who do the will of my father in heaven." And in Matthew 25, Jesus tells the parable of the sheep and the goats, in which those who act out their faith through charitable works are welcomed into heaven while those who only gave lip service to their faith are rejected. In the story of the wise and foolish builders, the story of the Good Samaritan, and the different talents, the faithful ones always perform positive faith-full actions while the unfaithful do nothing—even though with their lips they say they believe.

We should also stop for a moment and ask what happens when we do a good work. Let's say we pay a visit to a person in prison. The visit helps that person, but it also helps us. It is not a meaningless act of obedience to God. The action itself is worth something—it has done some good in the world. As such, it has changed us for the better, and therefore been a small step toward our becoming more Christ-like. Hebrews 11:1 says, "Faith is the substance of things hoped for, the evidence of things not seen," and when we do a faith-full good action we do just that—we give substance to the thing hoped for and that action becomes evidence for our unseen belief. The actions of faith which we complete through God's grace are a vital dimension to faith itself, and without them there is no faith at all.

How does this keep from becoming a religion in which we rely on good works to get us to heaven? The early church struggled with the relationship between faith and the Old Testament law. The early Christians were Jews and many of them thought they had to continue obeying all the Old Testament Rules and regulations. But St. Paul tried to make it clear that it was not by obeying the rules of the Old Testament law that we are saved. In the famous passage Ephesians 2:8–9, St. Paul says, "For it is by grace that you are saved through faith. It is the gift of God—not of works, lest any man should boast." St. Paul reminds the early church that they are saved not by obeying the Jewish law, but through faith. So he says in Romans 4:9–15, and he summarizes it in Romans 3:28 when he says, "For we maintain that a man is justified by faith apart from observing the law."

In these passages, St. Paul is not saying that faithful good works are unnecessary. Rather, he is saying that salvation does not come by obeying the Jewish law. In fact, Paul, like the rest of the New Testament writers, says clearly that we are destined to accomplish good works if we are people of faith. Right after the famous passage in Ephesians where he says that we have been saved by grace through faith, and not of works, he goes on to say, "For we are God's workmanship, created in Christ Jesus to do good works" (Eph. 2:10). In other words—just as the gospel taught—through faith we become one with Christ in order that we may speak his words and do his works in the world.

It is the epistle of James which ties all the strands from the gospels, St. Paul's letters and from the Old Testament together. In Chapter 2, James writes (2:14–24),

> What good is it, my brothers, if a man claims to have faith, but has no works? . . . Faith by itself, if it is not accompanied by action, is dead. You foolish man, do you want evidence that faith without deeds is useless? Was not our ancestor Abraham considered righteous for what he did when he offered his son Isaac on the altar? You see that his faith and his works were working together. . . . You see that a person is justified by what he does and not by faith alone.

In fact, there are not many Evangelicals who say that faith completely on its own is good enough. Most non-Catholics also recognize the need for good works to be present. They usually take the view that if the person is really united with Christ, then good works will be the fruit of that faith. John Calvin put it this way: "Salvation is by faith alone, but true faith is never alone." Much progress has been made in recent years in the attempt to find agreement between Protestants and Catholics on this issue. The biggest milestone has been the signing of the *Joint Declaration on Justification* between Catholics and Lutherans. Officials on the highest levels of the Catholic and Lutheran churches signed a statement on 31 October 1999. On the basis of this detailed theological statement, The Lutheran World Federation and the Catholic Church declared together that "the understanding of the doctrine of justification set forth in this declaration shows that a consensus in basic truths of the doctrine of justification exists between Lutherans and Catholics."[3]

In the sixteenth century both the Lutherans and the Catholics had condemned one another for their mutual doctrinal positions. Now both sides say,

> The teaching of the Lutheran Churches presented in the Declaration does not fall under condemnations from the Council of Trent. The condemnations in the Lutheran Confessions do not apply to the teaching of the Roman Catholic Church presented in this Declaration.[4]

---

3   *Common Statement*, 1; quoting *Joint Declaration*, 40.

4   *Joint Declaration*, 41.

The signing of this statement is a historic moment in the Church's life. Now we can say there is no formal reason why Protestants and Catholics should disagree over the doctrine of justification.

In the light of this formal agreement, both sides still need to continue explaining what they really do believe about salvation, and the relationship between our faith and our good works. Evangelicals admit that a person of faith will have to show his faith through the fruit of their lives, but they will still say that the good works themselves are not worth anything, and that they have nothing to do with the person's entrance into heaven. This is not quite what Catholics believe, and it is important to emphasize the differences—not to cause division and controversy, but because until the differences are brought out into the light and understood they can never be resolved.

In the *Joint Declaration on Justification*, Catholics and Lutherans both affirm that our faith and our good works are initiated and empowered by God's grace alone. But Catholics disagree with the extreme Protestant view that our good works are still worth nothing. That doesn't fit with common sense. Neither does it fit with the many passages of Scripture which show us being judged according to our works. Catholics admit that our good works can only be done through the power of God, but we also say the good works which we do in this way help to contribute to our final destiny. This is a little bit complicated, but it is vital to think it through. Catholics fully accept that our salvation was won for us by Christ's work on the cross and by his mighty resurrection. We accept his saving work through faith in him, and we can only take the step of faith through God's grace which empowers us. But our good works are worth something. Our good works are important for several vital reasons.

Firstly, our good or evil works are important for a very basic reason. How we choose to act is eternally important because our decisions and actions change things. This power to change things by our decision and action is called free will. Free will is actually God sharing some of his power with us to change the universe eternally. Now if our good decisions and actions are not worth anything, that means they cannot change things. If they do not change things, our decisions and actions are indeed meaningless. If this is true, then the feeling we get that things are changed is simply a huge illusion. If that is so, then the everything in the world which seems to occur by human decision and action is also an illusion, and we are all simply robots in a vast computer game which is pre-programmed. If this is true, that our decisions and actions are meaningless, then we actually do not have free will at all. This way of looking at things may protect faith from getting cluttered up with good works, but the problem is that if we do not have freedom to choose, then it is impossible for us to make any real choices at all. If we are not able to decide anything, then it is impossible for us to step out in faith in the first place. Logic insists that if we have the free will to make the step of faith, then we also have the free will to take other decisions and actions which affect our eternal destiny. On the other hand, if our decisions and actions have no power, then neither does our initial decision to follow Christ. Once we separate faith from works, both faith and works become impossible. It is only by keeping the two together that both become a reality.

The second reason good works are vitally important is because we have bodies. It is through our bodies that we can actually work out what we believe, and if we don't do this, then our faith remains a head and heart game. The Christian religion is not simply a good idea or an inspiring feeling. As they say, "love is a verb." So is Christianity. It is with our bodies that we live out the faith of our head and heart. The Docetists were early heretics who believed Christ only "seemed" to be human. Ignatius of Antioch noticed that this wrong belief about Jesus affected how they behaved. He wrote, "They have no concern for love, none for the widow, the orphan, the afflicted, the prisoner the hungry, the thirsty. They stay away from the Eucharist and prayer."[5]

The physical world is the stage on which we play out the drama of our salvation. This is vitally important because at the core of our faith is the belief that God himself took a human body and worked out our salvation through shedding his blood. Good works are physical, and God works through the physical. We can pray for the housebound widower next door, but only through our bodies can we get up out of a chair, bake a pie and take it around to his house.

The third reason good works matter is because it is through good works that our faith is perfected. Through discovery and learning, our faith matures into a deeper understanding. Through living the faith, the faith grows and matures. Through our attempts at good works, we learn just how difficult faith really is. Through our failures, we learn again and again how much we need to

---

5   Ignatius of Antioch, *Epistle to the Smyrnaeans*, 6.

rely on God's grace, and how much more we have yet to learn. Through our successful attempts, we understand what faith is really about at the very depths of our whole person. It is through our struggle to live out our faith that our faith comes to fullness and perfection. Through our good works the seedling of our faith grows strong and tall. Without those good works it remains a frail and tender shoot.

Let's say a child is extremely gifted musically. She has perfect pitch, she has an instinctive ear for melody and understands music with an amazing God-given talent. Her gift is extraordinary and wonderful and it will take her to the very top of her profession as a world class musician. Despite all this, the little girl still needs to practice. The practice isn't the talent, the practice cannot take the place of the talent, but without the practice the talent lies dormant. It is the practice that makes the talent live. It is the practice which gets rid of the imperfections, the mistakes and the human failures. It is the practice which makes perfect, as the old saying goes. The good works of worship, prayer and Christian action are the means by which Christ comes alive in us and by which we become fit for heaven. Through good works practice makes the perfect Christian.

Because of this, Catholics believe that good works are necessary. They are not necessary to earn our way into heaven; they are necessary to equip us for heaven. They are not necessary to please God, but to make us more like God. When we do something good, it actually accomplishes a real benefit in ourselves, in the world and in eternity. It is through our good works that we work with God to become more like his Son whose Spirit dwells within us. The good works are necessary because this process cannot be done in any other way. The good works are also necessary because by doing the good works, we engage our will. We get involved. God has given us free will, and through our good works we use it to keep our side of the bargain.

All through the Scripture, the heroes of faith are refined and purified by their actions of obedience. Through their obedience, pain and sacrifice they are brought to the perfection that God wills for them. The gospel says it is the pure in heart who see God and Jesus says in Mt. 5:48 that we are to be perfect as our father in heaven is perfect. It is the life of faith which brings us to this purity and perfection. Somewhere along the line, that life of faith includes discipline, self-sacrifice and suffering. Unless we take up our cross, Jesus says, we cannot be his disciple. God plans not only to save us, but to make us like his Son. This purification can only be done through God's power at work in us, but we have to co-operate with his power. Through our choices, our good works, and especially through our suffering, we work with God to grow towards wholeness.

If our good works and the difficult circumstances of life toughen and purify us, then these same disciplines help to weed out the sin in our lives. In other words, it is through our good works, discipline and sufferings that we can counter the effects of sin. What do I mean by this? Let's say we have stolen five hundred dollars from a neighbor. If we go to the neighbor and confess what we've done, he may very well forgive us, but he will quite rightly still expect us to pay back the five hundred dollars. Paying back the money will be a good deed, but it may cause us some pain. It takes a good deed and some suffering to counter the effects of the sin of stealing. It is the same in our relationship to God. God forgives the fact of our sin through Jesus Christ, but we are still responsible for the effects of our actions. We still have to deal with the fallout from sin. You might be forgiven for breaking a vase, but you still have to pick up the pieces.

Suffering is another way this process of purification can take place. Through suffering we identify with the painful consequences of sin, and by accepting suffering we can counter balance its deadly effect in our life. Jesus did this perfectly, as Hebrews 5:8–9 says: "Although he was a son he learned obedience from what he suffered, and once made perfect he became the source of eternal salvation for all who obey him." The same truth applies to us. In a wonderful passage at the beginning of Romans 5, St. Paul says how he is justified by faith, but he rejoices in suffering because it is suffering which brings him a deeper hope and identification with Christ. Suffering helps to purify us, but in a mysterious and exciting way the Scripture says our suffering may also help other people spiritually. So St. Paul writes to the Colossians, "Now I rejoice in what was suffered for you and I fill up in my flesh what is still lacking in regard to Christ's afflictions for the sake of his body which is the church" (Col. 1:24). In some mysterious way, our human good works, self-denial and suffering help to complete the work of Christ in the world. Good works and suffering are not just the empty fruit of our faith. As Hebrews says, they are the substance of our faith. Furthermore, good works and suffering have value in themselves. They actually have a spiritually beneficial effect on others. They change the world and they change us. They don't save us, but they make our faith real and through God's grace they can help to transform and purify us.

## *Getting Saved*

When I was five years old I came home from church one Sunday night and told my mother I wanted to get saved. I must have heard something in the sermon that prompted my young heart to realize its need. I can remember kneeling down with my mother, telling Jesus I was sorry for my sins and asking him to come into my heart. This simple act of repentance and faith was the basis for my Christian life. I was told that I was now "born again," that I was bound for heaven, and that nothing could take away my salvation. Being "born again" or "receiving Jesus Christ as your personal Lord and Savior" is the bedrock of the Evangelical experience. This personal relationship with Jesus Christ is a valuable and important contribution to the whole Church—both Catholic and Evangelical. My acceptance of Jesus when I was five years old was a good thing, and part of our evangelical teaching stressed that while my salvation was certain, I still had to grow in the faith. I needed to learn more about the Bible. I needed to pray, go to church and strive to obey the Lord's will for my life. In this way the whole evangelical system properly encouraged a life in which faith was worked out in the person's life.

I was told that because of my simple profession of faith, I was saved for all eternity. The Protestant view of justification gives the true impression that because of Jesus' work on the cross our salvation is accomplished for us. Different images are used for this. One of them is the judicial model which says God the Almighty Judge sees that justice is accomplished on the cross and so does not hold us guilty any longer. This is a valuable and good insight, and from the eternal perspective it is true. In one sense our salvation and perfection are already accomplished in Christ, but it is also true that it still our salvation needs to be "worked out in fear and trembling" (Phil. 2:12). Some forms of non-Catholic theology suggest that since our salvation is accomplished, there is nothing further we can do, and our status as children of God is written forever in the heavenly register.

Extreme views in this direction wind up taking away our free will and are contrary to the New Testament teaching. Grace may be at work in our life. We may have faith and choose to follow Christ. But if it is true that our free will may be used to choose Christ, it must also be true that the same free will may be used to deny Christ and turn away from him forever. The Book of Hebrews, which tells us so much about the life of faith, also tells us that our salvation is not signed, sealed and delivered for all eternity. Perseverance is needed if we are to finally enter the kingdom of God. Matthew 7:20 says trees that bear bad fruit will be thrown on the fire. The Book of Hebrews warns (10:26, 36):

> If we deliberately keep on sinning after we have received the knowledge of the truth no sacrifice of sins in left. . . . You need to persevere so that when you have done the will of God you will receive what he has promised.

In fact, Hebrews not only says one may fall away from faith, but it may be impossible for them to return (Heb. 6:4):

> It is impossible to restore again to repentance those who have once been enlightened, who have tasted the heavenly gift, and have become partakers of the Holy Spirit, . . if they then commit apostasy, since they crucify the Son of God on their own account and hold him up to contempt.

In verses 10 and 11 the writer stresses that the believer's faithful work is necessary for him to retain his salvation.

> God is not unjust; he will not forget your work and the love you have shown him as you have helped his people and continue to help them. We want each of you to show this same diligence to the very end, in order to make your hope sure.

Peter teaches the same thing. In 2 Peter 1:10–11 he says,

> Make every effort to add to your faith goodness, . . . therefore my brothers, be all the more eager to make your calling and election sure. For if you do these things you will receive a rich welcome into the eternal kingdom of our Lord and Savior Jesus Christ.

God created us in his image. Part of this truth means that when he gave us the power to choose, he gave each of us a tiny bit of his own power. We may choose to follow him to glory or we may choose to be separated from him forever. If we choose to open our lives to his grace, then we have a sure and certain hope of heaven. Furthermore, if we co-operate with God's grace, it gives us the power to be completely transformed. St. Paul sums up this confidence in 2 Corinthians 5:17–18 where he says, "Therefore if anyone is in Christ, he is a new creation; the old has passed away, behold, the new has come. All this is from God, who through Christ reconciled us to himself."

Some non-Catholic thinking says the new creation is a kind of legal fiction. It is said that God looks on our sinful condition and sees Jesus instead. To Luther is often attributed the statement that our condition was like "a dunghill covered with snow." Catholics don't accept this view. We believe Jesus' death and resurrection makes the new creation a real possibility—not just a legal fiction. Not only are we justified, but we are actually given the power to become the sons of God (Gal. 3:26; 4:6). The early Church fathers put it in a striking way—they said in Jesus God became man so that man could become like God. In other words, the real physical and historical event of the incarnation enables real physical and historical people like you and me to become like God.

Through faith, we are made just in God's eyes, but based on this fact Catholics believe we have the potential to actually become like Christ. This is not just something which will happen in heaven. We believe it can happen here and now. In St. John's first epistle he says the Christian is one who no longer sins. Is this really possible? The saints show us that it is. A saint is an ordinary person who has been totally transformed by grace. The saint has become all he was made to be through God's goodness. While Catholics recognize that this is hard work, we have also insisted from the earliest times that this is not something we can do on our own. St. Augustine said,

> Indeed we also work, but we are only collaborating with God who works, for his mercy has gone before us. It has gone before us so that we may be healed, and follows us so that once healed, we may be given life; it goes before us so that we may be called, and follows us so that we may be glorified; it goes before us so that we may live devoutly, and follows us so that we may always live with God: for without him we can do nothing.[6]

*More Christianity* fully affirms that we are saved through grace by faith, but it affirms more than that. The same grace that saves us through faith also

---

6   Augustine of Hippo, *On Nature and Grace*, 31.

enables us to live a victorious faith-full life. Furthermore, that grace which calls and saves us is available for our day-to-day walk with God in floods of blessing we can hardly imagine. This amazing grace is present in the world to bring us into the abundant life which Christ promised.

More Christianity affirms fully that we are saved by faith in Jesus Christ, but faith in Jesus Christ also means a daily life which is lived in his presence and power. By faith Christ lives in me and through my life. Through faith in Christ I can become a new incarnation of Christ in the world. Because of this amazing reality, what I say and do really matters. Because of this kind of faith, real people matter. Real choices matter. Real actions matter. If our decisions and actions matter, then there is everything to play for. We may lose our soul to gain the world, or we may lose the world and gain our soul. We may forfeit everything through our sinful choices, or we may inherit all things through faith in God's promises. If we work alongside God's grace, then we really can be healed. We really can become whole. We really can make an eternal difference. In Christ, our potential is enormous, and the challenge is exciting. More Christianity accepts the challenge. It works daily to move further up and further in to God's amazing new life. It builds on the foundation of our justification and co-operates with God's grace to become more and more like Christ himself. The possibility of perfection spurs us on to greater and greater devotion to the Lord who calls us to himself until, as St. Benedict says, "We run on the path of God's commandments with an inexpressible delight of love."[7]

This is a cause for great enthusiasm and supernatural joy. Knowing the possibilities of healing and transformation which grace provides, Therese of Lisieux encourages us to move forward with great zeal, saying, "You cannot be half a saint. You must be a whole saint or no saint at all!"[8]

Furthermore, this possibility of total transformation is not only for us. It is for the church and for the whole world. Jesus died to save not just my soul, but to redeem the whole fallen creation. If the possibility really exists that I can be transformed into his likeness, then the possibility also exists that, through his power, the whole church can continue to be transformed into his likeness. If I can be changed, that means the whole world can be changed. This

---

7  Benedict of Nursia, *Rule*, Prologue, 49.

8  Therese of Lisieux, *Letter to Abbe Belliere, 21 June 1897*.

is not simply a future reality in heaven. It means we can change ourselves and change the world right here and right now. As Christ's agents in the world we have the real power and responsibility to effect that transformation. This is why Christians are called to get involved in ministering to the sick and the poor, the uneducated and the downtrodden. The good news is that through faith real change is possible. It only depends how much we respond to God's grace in our lives.

That real change happens through the nitty gritty of our real ordinary lives. More Christianity is glorious, complex and majestic, but it is also humble, simple and plain. It is the religion of the incarnation where kings and shepherds meet, and where angels sing the praises of one born in a stable. Our justification by grace through faith enables us to gaze up to the stars with hope while keeping our feet firmly on the ground. Our good works are the physical outworking of our faith, and our faith is the elevation and glory of our good works. Through the two together, we get a glimpse of a God who reaches down to work within this physical realm. As he modelled the first man out of a lump of clay, so he is still getting his hands dirty granting us the gift of himself through our ordinary physical lives.

# BAPTISM NOW SAVES YOU

Even though I was brought up in a devoutly Evangelical home, I wasn't baptized until I was twenty-one years old. We attended an Independent Bible Church with an essentially Baptist theology. The irony about this Baptist theology is that it actually de-emphasized Baptism.

We were taught that Baptism, like the other sacraments, was inessential for our salvation. What mattered was whether or not we were "born again" or "saved." What mattered was whether we had responded to an altar call and "accepted Jesus into our hearts." This personal experience of repentance of faith was all that was necessary to assure us of eternal salvation. Baptism and communion, while they were not dispensed with altogether, remained unnecessary symbols of our inner faith.

I had responded to the appeal to accept Christ when I was just five years old. As a result, as I grew up, no one pressured me or even encouraged me to be baptized. When I became an Anglican as a college student, though, I had to submit to Baptism before I could be confirmed. Later I went to teach in a Christian school attached to a Baptist Church, and even then, the pastor seemed more concerned about the mode of Baptism than Baptism itself. He insisted that I be re-baptized by total immersion since he didn't think my Anglican Baptism (with water poured over my head) counted.

## *The "Romans Road"*

Having lived in England for twenty-five years, I had little opportunity to come across Baptists, and had forgotten about their very low view of the sacrament of Baptism. Now that our family has moved back to South Carolina, that is not the case. I was reminded of the Baptist beliefs some time ago, when two fundamentalist Baptists came around to discuss theology with me. They proceeded to take me along the famous "Romans Road." This is a simple Evangelical process that leads a person to salvation through the most basic Christian truths taken from St. Paul's epistle to the Romans.

The first verse is Romans 6:23, "For all have sinned and fallen short of the glory of God." After establishing that you are a sinner, the first part of the same verse reminds you that "the wages of sin is death." The last part of the verse gives the promise that "the gift of God is eternal life through Jesus Christ our Lord." Romans 5:8 tells us that "while we were yet sinners Christ died for us." Romans 10:13 says that "Whoever calls on the name of the Lord will be saved", and Romans 10:9 says that "If you confess with your mouth Jesus as Lord, and believe in your heart that God raised Jesus from the dead, you shall be saved."

This is all fine as far as it goes. What the Baptists' theology affirms is good: we need to acknowledge that we are sinners, that Jesus died to save us, and that we have to believe on him in our hearts and profess with our mouths that we believe. But like much Evangelical theology, it does not go far enough. Sometimes half the truth is the enemy of the truth. We need to look at the context of these admirable verses, and when we do, we discover that there is more to it than that.

My visitors took me through the Romans Road, and were a little nonplussed when I agreed with them on every point. I then asked them why they didn't go any further along the Romans Road. They asked what I meant. "St. Paul goes on to say just how this salvation happens," I replied. "He gives us an objective and solid way to know that we really have been made one with Christ. But first, we agree, don't we, that salvation means we die with Christ so that we may have new life?"

They agreed.

"How does this happen?" I asked.

"You have to accept Jesus. Believe on him in your heart and confess with your lips."

"Yes, we Catholics believe that this is necessary, but there is more to it than that. In addition to believing and confessing with our lips we need to be baptized. At the beginning of Romans 6, St. Paul actually says how we share in the death and new life of Christ: it is through Baptism."

We turned to the beginning of the sixth chapter of Romans to read, "don't you know that all of us who were baptized into Christ Jesus were baptized into his death? We were therefore buried with him through Baptism into death in order that, just as Christ was raised from the dead through the glory of the Father, we too may live a new life" (Rom. 6:3). We read the following verses, and I pointed out that this idea that we are made one with Christ through

Baptism is reiterated by Paul in Colossians 2:12, and in Galatians 3:27 he likens Baptism to "being clothed with Christ."

Furthermore, the fuller idea of salvation being a union with Christ fits with much more of the New Testament, which speaks time and again of being in a profound union with the living Lord—rather than simply being saved or justified by a personal belief in Christ.

The symbol and sacrament of Baptism therefore takes the believer from the simple repentance, belief and profession of faith into a more mysterious identification with Christ, in which he is the vine, and we are the branches, we die with him so that we might rise to new life. The necessity of Baptism is therefore not simply the need to add a meaningful symbol to the act of faith. It is an action which takes the believer's whole body, soul and spirit into a new relationship with God.

## *Peter and John*

The passage in Romans 6 (backed up by Colossians 2) is not the only evidence from the New Testament that Baptism is effective and therefore necessary for salvation. The Apostles Peter and John confirm St. Paul's teaching. In Acts 2:38, when St. Peter is preaching at Pentecost, his hearers ask what they must do to be saved, and he replies, "Repent and be baptized." In the third chapter of the first epistle of Peter, Noah's ark is referred to as a type of Baptism, and Peter writes (1 Pet. 3:21),

> In it only a few people, eight in all, were saved through water, and this water symbolizes Baptism that now saves you—not the removal of dirt from the body but the pledge of a good conscience toward God. It saves you by the resurrection of Jesus Christ.

The most famous New Testament evidence for the efficacy and necessity of Baptism is in John's gospel. When Nicodemus comes to visit Jesus by night, Jesus says that a person cannot enter the kingdom of God without being born again. Nicodemus asks how a man might enter again into his mother's womb and Jesus corrects him saying, "no one can enter the kingdom of heaven unless he is born of water and the Spirit" (Jn. 3:5). From the earliest days of the church this passage has been understood as referring to Baptism, and this interpretation is virtually unanimous down through history.

However, many Evangelicals have a peculiar interpretation for this verse. They say that the "water" in the verse does not refer to Baptism, but to the amniotic fluid of the mother's womb. This is the "water" that breaks at the point of physical birth. Therefore, they believe that when Jesus refers to "water and the Spirit," he is referring to physical birth and spiritual rebirth.

This might be a possible interpretation, as the previous verse was a discussion of a man entering again into his mother's womb. However, one must look at the whole passage in its context. It is universally agreed that John's gospel is the most "sacramental" in its approach. The passages of Jesus' life and teachings are put together in such a way as to connect with, and support, the sacramental life of the early church. In the verses that immediately follow Jesus' words that one must be "born again of water and the Spirit" (3:5), Jesus talks about the "wind blowing where it wills" (Jn. 3:8) and then goes on to talk about "men loving darkness rather than light because their deeds are evil" (3:19), and that whoever "lives by the truth comes to the light" (3:21). The references to light and the wind blowing where it wills are clear references to the other main symbols of the baptismal ceremony—the wind and the lighted candle. If there is any doubt, the very next story in John chapter three shows Jesus immediately going out with his disciples baptizing.

## *Yes, but . . .*

As soon as you begin to speak about the necessity of Baptism, an Evangelical will pull out some favorite verses and favorite arguments. They will go back to Romans 10:9–10,

> If you confess with your mouth, 'Jesus is Lord,' and believe in your heart that God raised him from the dead, you will be saved. For it is with your heart that you believe and are justified, and it is with your mouth that you confess and are saved.

They will point out that this verse does not say that one must be baptized. The reply is that belief and profession of faith are necessary, but the whole witness of the New Testament shows us that Baptism is necessary as well.

Evangelicals may also refer to the story of the Philippian jailer in Acts 16. The jailer cries out, "What must I do to be saved?" and Paul and Silas reply, "Believe on the Lord Jesus Christ and you will be saved—you and your household" (16:31). It seems there is no demand for Baptism. However, actions speak louder than words because the next verse says that "immediately they were baptized" (16:33). Baptism therefore seems to be the way one makes the faith commitment. This is just one example from the Acts of the Apostles where faith is accompanied by Baptism, and it is assumed that both are necessary. Two other clear accounts are Philip's encounter with the Ethiopian Eunuch in Acts 8, and Peter's immediate Baptism of Cornelius and his household in Acts 10. The pattern in Acts is consistent: preaching, repentance of the hearers, belief in Christ and immediate Baptism. Why would this be the case if the apostles did not believe that Baptism was both effective and necessary for Baptism?

## *Yes, but still . . .*

The Evangelical who is still not convinced of the efficacy and necessity of baptism may pose a few more difficulties. What about people who do not have the opportunity to be baptized? He will bring up the good thief on the cross. "Look here," he protests, "the thief couldn't be baptized, but Jesus says, "Today you will be with me in paradise" (Lk. 23:43). This is the perfect opportunity to explain two other aspects of Catholic belief. First of all, it should be explained that the Catholic Church does not believe that Baptism is magic and that simply by having water poured over one's head with the Trinitarian formula, a person is instantly saved forever. Baptism incorporates the individual into the Body of Christ, and within the whole life of the Church an individual's Baptism must be accompanied by faith.

The developing faith of the individual is empowered by the grace of Baptism, and nurtured by the whole Church, but if the Christian faith is rejected or never positively affirmed, the Baptism is not magically effective.

To cover the difficult cases, it should be explained that the Catholic Church has always taught "Baptism of blood" and "Baptism of desire." The first means that individuals who were never baptized, but gave their life in martyrdom for Christ, are incorporated, through their own death, into the mystical body of Christ through a mystical sharing in his sacrificial death.

"Baptism of desire" applies to those individuals with faith in Christ, who would be baptized if they had the opportunity and if they truly understood what Baptism means. "Baptism of desire" not only applies to those who, due to extraordinary circumstances, do not have access to water for Baptism. The New Testament indicates that what we call "Baptism of desire" is the case for the Old Testament saints. Noah and his family were "saved through water" in the flood (1 Peter 3:8), and the Hebrew children were baptized "into Moses in the cloud and the Red Sea" (1 Cor. 10:2). This suggests that Baptism of desire may also extends to those who have pre-Christian faith, or to non-Christians who have faith according to the level of their knowledge, but have never heard the Christian gospel.

It may also apply to those who have faith in Christ, but have not been baptized because they truly and sincerely (because of false teaching received in good faith) do not believe that Baptism is necessary. Even in these cases, however, it should be understood that the Church teaches that such individuals may be saved, not that they necessarily are saved.

## *The Sacramental Economy*

The most difficult thing for an Evangelical to accept in a conversation about the sacraments, is that God actually uses physical means and liturgical ceremonies to dispense his grace and administer salvation. The typical Evangelical is heavily conditioned to dismiss all physical components of religion as useless and distracting "manmade traditions."

However, the Evangelicals' theory doesn't stand up to their own practice. It cannot, because they have bodies that are in time and space. They therefore need a way to respond physically to spiritual realities. It is not very difficult to show a good Evangelical that they actually believe that physical actions and religious ceremonies can be at least useful for salvation—otherwise why do they have evangelistic rallies with emotional music and extended "altar calls?" Why do they encourage people to "put up their hand, get up out of their seat and come forward?" It's because they realize that we need physical actions, religious ceremonies and rituals to help us accept the gift of salvation that is being offered, and they must accept that it is through these physical responses that salvation is accepted, and that the physical responses are therefore effective and necessary.

If they can see that God uses their preaching and their traditions and religious rituals to bring people to salvation, then it is not too much of a leap for them to see that the Catholic rituals are another physical and active way for individuals to accept the gift of salvation. Of course, the sacraments are more than a practical, manmade religious tool. The sacraments are not done by us for God, but by God for us. However, moving a non-Catholic to the point where he accepts that a sacrament is useful is the first step towards accepting that it is necessary, and that is just one step away from the acceptance that they are not just man-made practical religious devices, but divinely instituted initiatives that incorporate the soul into the mystical Body of Christ.

An Answer *Not* An Argument / Fr. Dwight Longenecker

# WHAT DO WE MEAN BY THE REAL PRESENCE?

"But I believe in the Real Presence!" said Doug, my Bible Christian friend, "Why do you Catholics refuse to admit me to communion?"

"Whoa!" I said, "I'm delighted to hear that you believe in the Real Presence, but what do you actually mean by the term?"

"Well, I prefer to remain vague about the details," said Doug. "I would only want to go as far as the Scriptures do, and St. Paul says in 1 Corinthians that the communion is "a sharing in the body of Christ." I don't think you have to go further than that."

We then sparred through John 6 and 1 Corinthians 11; but the conversation got me thinking about the term "real presence." Doug was happy to use the term to describe what he felt about the Lord's Supper at his independent Bible Church. It was during my Anglican days that I'd got used to the phrase "real presence." Anglo-Catholics used the term all the time, and even many evangelical Anglicans seem fairly happy to use "real presence" to describe their view of the Eucharist. But then I picked my brain a bit further and remembered Methodists, Reformed ministers and other free evangelicals using the term as well. When I became a Catholic I found lots of Catholics also using the term "real presence" to refer to their Eucharistic beliefs.

But what did everyone mean by the term? Could it be that God was using the term "real presence" as a kind of ecumenical bridge? Was it becoming a universally accepted term which was bringing non-Catholics into the fold of the true church? I didn't want to rule out this creative possibility, but I had my suspicions that "real presence" was in fact, an elastic term which could mean almost anything, and was therefore the enemy of true ecumenism.

So, for instance, a Bible Christian might mean by "real presence" something like "I feel closer to Jesus at the Lord's Supper." At the same time a Methodist might mean, "When we gather together the presence of the Lord is real among us"—referring simply to our Lord's promise that "Where two or three are gathered together, there am I in their midst." A Lutheran might mean Christ's risen presence is "with" or "beside" the bread and wine. An Anglican evangelical might say, "There is a real sense in which Christ is present as the church gathers—for the Church too is the Body of Christ." At the same time an Anglo-Catholic would say there is a real, objective abiding spiritual presence of Christ when the Eucharist is celebrated.

One of the reasons the term "real presence" has become a flexible friend is that it has been lifted from its full context. Historically, theologians spoke of "the real presence of Christ's body and blood in the sacrament of the altar." But now it has been shortened to "the real presence." Reference to the body and blood has been quietly dropped and even the name of Christ is omitted. As a result, for some people, "real presence" has come to mean simply "the idea of the risen Lord" or "the Spirit of Christ" or even just the "fellowship of the church." In fact, the term "the real presence" could mean just about anything to anybody. There are probably even some New Agers who talk about the "real presence" of the Christ within.

Another reason why the term is so conveniently vague is because "real presence" in most usage focuses on the abstract noun "presence" and not on the body and blood of Christ. This implies that the "presence" is somehow separate from the sacrament.

The widespread use of this term is a sign that many non-Catholics are coming around to a higher view of the sacrament. This is cause for rejoicing. But it is also a cause for concern because a lot of non-Catholics—on hearing Catholics use the term—quite innocently assume that Catholics believe the same thing they do. Thus, a Bible Baptist might use the term "real presence" as meaning he "feels closer to Jesus at communion" and hearing Catholics use the term, concludes that Catholics believe the same thing about the Eucharist as he does. As a result—like my friend Doug—he can't understand why he is not welcome to receive communion at a Catholic Mass. So while the widespread use of the term "real presence" seems encouraging, it's really misleading. The ambiguous terminology causes confusion and encourages false ecumenism. But so far, my theory was only a hunch.

I decided to do a bit of research. I travelled to Downside Abbey—the great Benedictine house in the Southwest of England. After Mass, the librarian Fr. Daniel ushered me from the neo-Gothic monastic buildings over to the library, which looks like a newly-landed flying saucer. I wanted to discover more about this term "real presence." I wanted to find out when the term was first used and why. I figured that finding out the background of the term might explain why and how it was being used today.

My first port of call was the Oxford Dictionary of the Christian Church. They defined "real presence" as an especially Anglican term which "emphasized the real presence of the body and blood of Christ at the Eucharist as contrasted with others that maintain that the Body and Blood are present only figuratively or symbolically." The first edition of the dictionary quoted the sixteenth century English reformer Latimer to show his use of the term: "this same presence may be called most fitly a real presence, that is, a presence not feigned, but a true and faithful presence."

That sounded pretty Catholic, but then it became a bit more complicated because the second edition of the same dictionary points out that the English Reformers only used the phrase with other expressions which made it a term for receptionism—the belief that the bread and wine only become the body and blood of Christ to those who receive it faithfully. So Latimer is quoted in the second edition more fully: "that same presence may be called a real presence because to the faithful believer there is a real or spiritual body of Christ."

But Catholics believe in a corporeal, substantial presence of Christ in the Eucharist. The whole Christ is present, body, blood soul and divinity. It is not just a spiritual presence. Furthermore, Catholics believe in an objective presence—not one which is only available to those who receive in faith. Latimer's colleague Ridley makes the Anglican position about the real presence most clear. Writing in the Oxford Disputations of 1554 he says,

> The true Church [sic] doth acknowledge a presence of Christ's body in the Lord's Supper to be communicated to the godly by grace . . . spiritually and by a sacramental signification, but not as a corporeal presence of the body of his flesh.[1]

This seemed to be the root of the term. It was a construction of the English Reformation. Latimer and Ridley did their best to come up with a term for the Eucharist which would please their Catholic persecutors and yet not compromise their Protestant beliefs. But maybe there was more to it. What if the term "real presence" actually originated before the sixteenth century?

---

1   Foxe, *Acts and Monuments* (London, 1684), 61.

Fr. Daniel brought me an excellent two-volume work, *The History of the Doctrine of the Holy Eucharist*, by Oxford scholar Darwell Stone.[2] In this wonderful book, Stone traces the church's beliefs about the Eucharist from New Testament times through the late nineteenth century. The book is arranged chronologically with copious quotations from the various theologians.

Debates over the body and blood of Christ in the sacrament really blew up with the eleventh century French theologian Berengar of Tours. Berengar denied that there could be a material change at the consecration, and the controversy raged for the next two hundred years, ending in the definition of transubstantiation at the Fourth Lateran Council in 1215. It is interesting that during this controversy the orthodox terminology is "real body and real blood of Christ." The term "real presence" doesn't occur.

I found the first reference to the term "real presence" in the fourteenth century theologian John of Paris. He wrote, "I intend to defend the real and actual presence of the body of Christ in the Sacrament of the Altar, and that it is not there only as by way of a sign . . . ." But John of Paris was deprived of his professorship because his views on the sacrament were considered unorthodox. It was in the same century that the precursor of Latimer and Ridley, John Wycliffe, also used the term "real presence." Like Ridley and Latimer, he used "real presence" as an alternative to transubstantiation. In other words, "real presence" was a compromise term used to suggest a high view of the sacrament while in fact denying the Catholic doctrine of transubstantiation.

As I'd already suspected, the same position was held by Ridley and Latimer who also searched for a compromise term. They denied transubstantiation, and held a merely symbolic and spiritual view of the sacrament, but they wanted to avoid extreme Zwingli-ism and because of Catholic pressure needed to express their beliefs in as high a way as possible. Thus, Ridley and Latimer said they believed in the real presence; but this was simply their term for a kind of high receptionism.

So the term "real presence" has—from the start—been used as an alternative to the Catholic doctrine of transubstantiation. Not only did Latimer and Ridley use "real presence" to deny transubstantiation, but so did

---

2    Darwell Stone, *A History of the Doctrine of the Holy Eucharist*, 2 vols. (London: Longmans, Green & Co., 1909).

the seventeenth century "high church" Anglican divine Jeremy Taylor (1613–1667) who used the term "real presence" as a contrast to transubstantiation in his treatise, *The Real and Spiritual Presence of Christ in the Blessed Sacrament proved against the Doctrine of Transubstantiation*.

Stone's second volume of shows how the great Anglican, E. B. Pusey, re-coined the phrase "real presence" in the mid-nineteenth century and promoted it most strongly. It is thanks to Pusey that the term entered common usage within the Oxford movement and eventually made its way through the Anglican and other non-Catholic churches to be used so widely today.

But what did Pusey mean by "the real presence"? He was at pains to point out that he did not hold to any corporeal presence of Christ in the Eucharist. "In the communion there is a true, real actual though spiritual communication of the body and blood of Christ to the believer through the holy elements." In another place Pusey denies transubstantiation explicitly and argues for a "mystical, sacramental and spiritual presence of the body of our Lord." And most explicitly, in 1857 Pusey says, "there is no physical union of the body and blood of Christ with the bread and wine."

Pusey in the Oxford of the mid-1850s was not at risk of being burned at the stake like Ridley and Latimer. But in that same university city he felt a similar pressure of trying to reconcile English reformation doctrines with the beliefs of the Catholic church. Pusey was under pressure because he sincerely wanted the Anglican church to be as Catholic as possible, but as an Anglican clergyman he had to subscribe to the Thirty-nine Articles of religion, and Article 28 specifically repudiates transubstantiation. So Pusey couldn't hold to transubstantiation even if he wanted to.

So, like Ridley and Latimer before him, he used the term "real presence" to sound as close to Catholicism as possible while in fact rejecting Catholic doctrine. Pusey believed the "real presence" of Christ in the sacrament was only a spiritual and sacramental presence. In this way the Victorian Anglo-Catholic actually agreed with the reformer Ridley who wrote, "The blood of Christ is in the chalice . . . but by grace and in a sacrament. . . . This presence of Christ is wholly spiritual."

So why does it matter if the presence is only spiritual and sacramental? It matters because the whole work of Christ is more than spiritual. It is physical. Ever since Irenaeus, the Catholic Church has been insistent that the incarnation really was a supernatural union of the spiritual and the physical. As Darwell Stone writes, Irenaeus was countering Gnosticism, "which interposed an insuperable barrier between spiritual beings and material things; between the true God of the universe and the universe of matter."[3] And it is one of the great heresies of our age that Christians attempt to "spirit away" the physicalness of the gospel. So the resurrection, the miracles and the incarnation itself become mere "spiritual events."

So likewise, the church has always insisted—despite the difficulties—that the presence of Christ in the Blessed Sacrament is not simply spiritual and subjective. It is objective and corporeal. In some way it is physical. The Fourth Lateran Council that explained that belief with the term transubstantiation. As the Oxford Dominican, Fr. Herbert McCabe has said, "Transubstantiation is not a complete explanation of the mystery, but it is the best description of what we believe happens at the consecration."

So what should Catholics do when confronted with this confusing term "real presence"? First of all Catholics should realize that it is not a Catholic term at all. Its history is mostly Anglican, and as such, it was always used as a way to adroitly sidestep the troublesome doctrine of transubstantiation; and as such, it is not an accurate term to describe true Catholic Eucharistic doctrine.

Secondly, when non-Catholics say they believe in the real presence, Catholics should ask what they mean by it. A non-Catholic will almost never mean transubstantiation. By the term "real presence" the non-Catholic most certainly does not mean he believes the sacrament is the body, blood, soul and divinity of our Lord. Asking what the non-Catholic means by the term "real presence" should be done in a positive and constructive way. Their definition can open the way for an explanation of what a Catholic means by "real presence." Clear definitions help everybody.

In his 1965 encyclical *Mysterium Fidei*, Pope Paul VI encourages the use of clear and unambiguous language about the Eucharist. He says,

> Having safeguarded the integrity of the faith it is necessary to safeguard also its proper mode of expression, lest by careless use of

---

[3] Darwell Stone, *A History of the Doctrine of the Holy Eucharist* (London: Longmans, Green & Co., 1909), 1:34.

words we occasion the rise of false opinions regarding faith in the most sublime of mysteries.[4]

In the same encyclical, Pope Paul actually uses the term "Real Presence" but he does so to outline the ways in which Christ is present in his church. Interestingly, Paul VI affirms all the ways non-Catholics might define "the real presence." He says Christ is really present in the church when she prays. He is also present when she performs acts of mercy. Christ is present in the church as she struggles to perfection. He is really present when the church governs the people of God. Christ is present in the preaching of the gospel and he is present as the church faithfully celebrates the Eucharist.

However, Paul VI also makes it clear that the Eucharistic presence of the body and blood of Christ is different from these other forms of Christ's presence. It is a unique presence. So he affirms,

> This presence is called "real" by which it is not intended to exclude all other types of presence as if they could not be "real" too, but because it is presence in the fullest sense. That is to say, it is a substantial presence by which Christ the God-Man is wholly and entirely present. It would therefore be wrong to explain this presence by taking resource to the "spiritual" nature, as it is called, of the glorified Body of Christ which is present everywhere, or by reducing it to a kind of symbolism as if this most august sacrament consisted of nothing else than an efficacious sign of the spiritual presence of Christ and of his intimate union with the Faithful members of his mystical body.[5]

So as Catholics, we must use clear language about the sacrament. We can affirm the "real" presence of Christ which non-Catholics affirm in the fellowship of the church, in the preaching of the gospel and in the celebration of the Eucharist, but we must also affirm that the fullest sense of the "real presence" is that which we worship in the Blessed Sacrament of the altar.

Although Paul VI used the term "real presence" in *Mysterium Fidei*, the whole thrust of the encyclical is to support and recommend the continued use of the term "transubstantiation" as the Catholic terminology. With this in mind, I suggest Catholics should avoid the ambiguous term "real presence"

---

4   Paul VI, *Mysterium Fidei*, 23.

5   Paul VI, *Mysterium Fidei*, 39.

and speak boldly of transubstantiation. Instead of "real presence" we should also use the terminology used in the twelfth century when the doctrine of transubstantiation was being hammered out. Then there was no talk of a vaguely spiritual "real presence;" instead they referred to the "real body and real blood of Christ."

*Mysterium Fidei* encourages those devotions which are implied by our belief in the "real body and real blood of Christ." That such devotions are encouraged as a support to transubstantiation is nothing new. It is no coincidence that just fifty years after the doctrine of transubstantiation was promulgated by the Fourth Lateran Council, Pope Urban IV decreed the Feast of Corpus Christi. The beliefs of the church are always reflected in her devotions. So we should encourage the devotions which accompany our belief in Christ's corporeal presence in the sacrament of the altar. It is the practice of benediction, prayer before the sacrament and veneration of the blessed sacrament which make clear exactly what we do mean by the term "real presence" and that it is not the same thing that non-Catholic Christians mean when they use the same term.

These distinctions should not be emphasized in a spirit of division and exclusion, but with the true longing for Christ's body to be reunited. That true and costly re-union will not come as long as we accept ambiguous language which allows us to pretend that we all believe the same thing. Instead it will come as we recognize the true divisions which still exist, understand our differences and seek to resolve them with patience, love and a good sense of humor.

# *How Do You Solve a Problem Like Maria?*

## DO CATHOLICS HONOR MARY TOO MUCH?

What do you do when a Protestant Christian challenges Catholic devotion to Mary as being excessive and distorted? My favorite correspondent came up with some Catholic quotes that were real showstoppers. Among others he quoted Pope Pius IX who, in *Ubi Primum*, wrote these words in praise of Mary:

> From our earliest years nothing has ever been closer to our heart than devotion—filial, profound, and wholehearted—to the most blessed Virgin Mary. Always have We endeavored to do everything that would redound to the greater glory of the Blessed Virgin, promote her honor, and encourage devotion to her . . . . Great indeed is Our trust in Mary. The resplendent glory of her merits, far exceeding all the choirs of angels, elevates her to the very steps of the throne of God. Her foot has crushed the head of Satan. Set up between Christ and His Church, Mary, ever lovable and full of grace, always has delivered the Christian people from their greatest calamities and from the snares and assaults of all their enemies, ever rescuing them from ruin. . . . The foundation of all Our confidence, as you know well, Venerable Brethren, is found in the Blessed Virgin Mary. For, God has committed to Mary the treasury of all good things, in order that everyone may know that through her are

obtained every hope, every grace, and all salvation. For this is His will, that we obtain everything through Mary.[1]

My Protestant friend made the point that if Pius IX's references to Mary were replaced by references to Jesus Christ, the quote would be uncontroversially Christian. As it is, he protested, it says things of Mary that should be said only of God. Was it true that nothing was closer to Pius IX's heart than devotion to Mary? Could it be true that the "foundation of all [his] confidence" is Mary? Is it really through her that we obtain "every hope, every grace and all salvation"?

On the face of it, this is rather difficult to answer. Pius IX's words *do* seem excessive.

But when you put them into context, the emphasis changes. First of all, the quotation in question is part of Pius IX's letter to the world bishops consulting with them about the wisdom of defining the dogma of the Immaculate Conception. In other words, he is speaking within a Marian document. Second, Pius IX is expressing his own opinion and love for Mary. He is not making a formal doctrinal pronouncement. Third, this statement has to be placed within the context of the whole worship and life of the church. Taken on its own, it sounds like Pius IX worships Mary. Taken in its context, it's clear that he doesn't. When the words are read closely it is clear that he is referring ultimately to Jesus Christ. He is the foundation who is found "in Mary." Jesus Christ is the one who is the source for "every hope, every grace and all salvation" and he comes to us through Mary.

Pius IX's words can be explained, but there are two underlying points to remember when discussing Marian devotion with non-Catholics. First of all, if we are confronted with florid language about the Blessed Virgin we mustn't apologize. Devotion to Mary has been part of the worship of the Church from the earliest days. There are many examples of what might seem like excessive language about Mary from the first centuries of the church. Here is just one sample from the fourth century writings of Athanasius:

> O noble Virgin, truly you are greater than any other greatness. For who is your equal in greatness, O dwelling place of God the Word? To whom among all creatures shall I compare you, O Virgin? You are

---

[1] Pius IX, Ubi Primum, 4–5.

greater than them all. O [Ark of the New] Covenant, clothed with purity instead of gold! You are the Ark in which is found the golden vessel containing the true manna, that is, the flesh in which divinity resides. Should I compare you to the fertile earth and its fruits? You surpass them . . . . If I say that heaven is exalted, yet it does not equal you . . . . If we say that the cherubim are great, you are greater than they, for the cherubim carry the throne of God while you hold God in your hands.[2]

Protestant Christians look to Athanasius as a hero of the faith. He's the one who defended orthodoxy against the heretics. He's the one who stood up against the whole world in defense of the Christology that Protestant Christians embrace today. If some Christians object to Catholic veneration of Mary as being excessive or distorted, then they are not only disagreeing with Pope Pius IX in 1849 but also with Athanasius in the fourth century.

Furthermore, proper devotion to the Blessed Virgin was considered to be a sign of a proper understanding of the Incarnation and a full devotional life for Jesus Christ. It may not be those who honor Mary, but those who neglect her who are distorting the historic faith. Those who dishonor Mary should pay attention to Epiphanius who also writes from the fourth century that "who dishonors the holy vessel [Mary] also dishonors his Master."[3]

The main problem with the Protestant criticism of Catholic devotion to Mary is their basic mindset. They see the whole question in terms of "either-or," not "both-and." Because Catholics venerate Mary, non-Catholics assume that this devotion must take the place of proper devotion to the Lord Jesus. A powerful analogy can be used to show non-Catholics how strange this seems to Catholics.

If an Evangelical Christian believes that devotion to Mary replaces proper devotion to Jesus, ask him to imagine what it would be like if he discovered that another Christian group thought Evangelicals were in grave error because of their emphasis on the Bible. Ask him to imagine that these fictional Christians accuse Evangelicals of neglecting Jesus because of their devotion to the Bible.

---

2   Athanasius of Alexandria, *Homily of the Papyrus of Turin*. Quoted in Luigi Gambero, *Mary and the Fathers of the Church: The Blessed Virgin Mary in Patristic Thought* (Ignatius Press, 1999), 106–7.

3   Quoted in Gambero, 127.

These hypothetical Christians say, "You evangelicals stress the Bible to the neglect of Jesus. You call your churches 'Bible' churches and have 'Bible' colleges instead of 'Christian' churches and colleges. Inside your church you don't have pictures of Jesus, you don't have any crucifixes; and you don't have the Stations of the Cross. Instead, all you have is a big central pulpit to preach the Bible."

The accusers could go on and point out that "The New Testament says the early Christians . . . devoted themselves . . . to the breaking of the bread" (Acts 2:42) and that the way to remember Jesus and proclaim his death is through the Eucharist (1 Cor. 11:24–26); yet you Evangelicals have the Lord's Supper once a month, or even less often, and the main feature of your church service is a long Bible sermon. You have removed the cross of Christ and replaced it with the Bible."

These accusers say, "You Evangelicals even have a formal doctrine named *Sola Scriptura*. This man-made dogma is a later distortion and addition to the Christian faith, something that is unheard of both in the Scriptures themselves and in the early church. This dogma (which you treat as infallible) states that the Bible and not Jesus is the only source of Truth. You teach your children to memorize Bible verses instead of receiving Jesus in communion. You teach them to sing, "The B-I-B-L-E, / Yes that's the book for me. / I stand alone on the word of God . . . ." Notice how they are not to stand alone on the sure foundation of Jesus Christ (1 Cor. 3:11), but on the Bible instead! Evangelical preachers say that there is no way anyone can come to God without believing the Bible. They declare their undying love for the Bible instead of Jesus. They say how their lives are totally dedicated to preaching the Bible instead of the cross of Christ.

If someone were to make this charge, a good Evangelical might well snort with dismay and bewilderment. How could someone so misunderstand his position? Surely, they are doing it on purpose! The good Evangelical would patiently explain to his critic, "You have misunderstood completely. *Sola Scriptura* doesn't set the Bible in opposition to Jesus. It does exactly the opposite: it helps us to glorify Jesus. Don't you see that we love the Bible because it gives us access to our Savior? It's true that we believe people need to know the Bible, but that's because the written Word and the incarnate Word are inextricably intertwined. You can't have one without the other. It is really Jesus we worship and proclaim through the Bible. If you just look at our whole practice and teaching with an open mind you would see how misguided and mistaken you really are."

But the critic of the Evangelical won't have it. He replies, "No, no. That all sounds very plausible, but you will never convince me. I just know that you worship the Bible instead of Jesus, and all your clever wordplay just goes to show how blind you really are."

To prove his point, the critic then says, "I know you Evangelicals worship the Bible instead of Jesus. Just look at this quotation I found that proves it. This comes from an Evangelical in one of your classic theological textbooks:

> The Bible . . . has produced the highest results in all walks of life. It has led to the highest type of creations in the fields of art, architecture, literature, and music. . . . [Y]ou will find everywhere the higher influence of the Bible. . . . William E. Gladstone said, "If I am asked to name the one comfort in sorrow, the sole rule of conduct, the true guide of life, I must point to what in the words of a popular hymn is called "the old, old story," told in an old, old Book, which is God's best and richest gift to mankind."[4]

"You see," the critic continues with a flourish, "your famous Evangelical leader says that it is not Jesus, but the Bible that is his 'one comfort', his 'true guide', and 'God's best and richest gift to mankind?' It just shows that Evangelicals worship the Bible and not the Lord."

Of course, this is a ridiculous distortion of the Evangelical view, but the extended analogy may help Protestants understand how Catholics feel when Protestants make similarly extreme charges about the Catholic devotion to Mary.

In the face of such charges, Catholics reply, "Are you serious? How can you possibly make such a fundamental and basic mistake about what we believe? We don't venerate Mary on her own, but because she has given us our Savior and because she constantly leads us to him. If you took time to study our whole teaching and practice you will see how this is true."

In debate with non-Catholics, we should admit that some Catholics may overemphasize Mary, just as some Evangelicals may take extreme views on the Bible. But we should also admit that both Catholics and Protestants warn

---

4 Henry Clarence Thiessen, *Introductory Lectures in Systematic Theology* (Wm. B. Eerdmans Publishing, 1949), 86.

against such dangers, and as we ask them to understand our point of view, we should also try to honestly understand theirs.

# EXPLAINING MARY, CO-REDEMPTRIX, TO AN EVANGELICAL

My first personal encounter with the Blessed Virgin Mary happened while I was a student at an Evangelical Anglican seminary in England. I had been brought up as an Evangelical and found my way into the Anglican church. There I was preparing for ordination. A Catholic friend who was a Benedictine oblate suggested that I might like to visit a Catholic Benedictine monastery.

While there, I told one of the monks that during a time of contemplative prayer I had sensed God's presence in a very real, but feminine way. The femininity disturbed me, because I knew God isn't feminine. The monk smiled and said, "Don't worry. That's not God. It's the Virgin Mary. She is the Mediatrix. She wants to help you with your prayers and bring you closer to God."

I was shocked. At the time, the Virgin Mary played no part in my devotional life. As a good Evangelical boy, I had memorized 1 Timothy 2:5, which says, "There is one mediator between God and man, the man Christ Jesus." Calling Mary "Mediatrix" confirmed my prejudice that Catholics believe things that contradicted the Bible. It also confirmed my suspicion that Catholics gave Mary an equal status with Jesus.

I put this notion firmly to one side and didn't consider it again until after I had come into the Catholic Church. This postponement was possible because Mary's role as co-redeemer and Mediatrix of grace is not a formally defined dogma of the Catholic Church. It remains a pious opinion—a useful devotional and theological way of meditating on Mary. My attention was not drawn back to the question until some years later, when I was writing *Mary: A Catholic/Evangelical Debate* with an old friend who had attended Bob Jones University with me.

## *A Stick to Beat Us With*

I understand how Mary's titles of Mediatrix and Co-Redemptrix remain one of the sorest points in Evangelical-Catholic discussions. A Protestant who has heard of these titles will use them as a big stick with which to beat Catholics, and it is important to know how best to engage the discussion.

For genuine dialogue, it is vital to listen to and understand the Evangelical point of view. The sincere, well-read Evangelical objects to exalted devotions and titles for the Mother of God because he thinks they detract from the honor and worship due to Jesus Christ alone. A thoughtful Evangelical does not intentionally despise Mary; he sidelines the Mother of God to defend the proper devotion to her Son.

The place to start in any discussion of Mary as Mediatrix and Co-Redemptrix is to affirm that Catholics indeed believe that the death of Jesus Christ is all-sufficient for the salvation of our sins. If you can quote an author who insists that Christ's death is all sufficient, but is also is a known devotee of Mary, it packs a stronger punch. "See, here's someone who promotes Marian devotion," you say, "He actually wants her to be proclaimed Co-Redemptrix, even though he fully understands that Chris's death is all-sufficient."

For example, a booklet by the California-based organization *Vox Populi Mariae Mediatrici*, which promotes these titles for Mary, begins with these words:

> The salvation of humanity was accomplished by God's only begotten Son, Jesus Christ. The Passion and Death of Christ, our sole Redeemer, was not only sufficient but 'superabundant' satisfaction for human guilt and the consequent debt of punishment.[1]

The booklet goes on to explain, "But God willed that this work of salvation be accomplished through the collaboration of a woman, while respecting her free will (Gal. 4:4)." This point introduces a good next step in discussing this Catholic belief with an Evangelical.

## *Will You Cooperate or Not?*

Instead of wading into an argument about Mary being Mediatrix and Co-Redemptrix, it is useful to discuss the principle and possibility of humans cooperating with God in the work of redemption. Protestants have a deeply ingrained resistance to the idea that we can cooperate with God for our redemption at all. In their desire to maintain the doctrines of *sola gratia* and *sola fide*, some of them go to the extremes of believing that we can do nothing

---

[1] "New Marian Dogma? Coredemptrix, Mediatrix of All Graces, Advocate."

at all to cooperate with God in our redemption, because to do so would be tantamount to salvation by works.

As a result, most Evangelical belief systems contain a very strong element of Quietism. Quietism is a sort of fatalism: It is that heresy which says you can do absolutely nothing to engage in the work of your salvation. Instead, each soul is like a leaf on the tide of God's almighty Providence. Because of this understanding, it is difficult for many Evangelicals to comprehend the idea that God uses human cooperation to accomplish his will in the world. That human cooperation is actually crucial to the Redemption of the world is not part of their perspective.

Therefore, before talking about Mary's collaboration with God, it is worth discussing the basic principle that humans can cooperate with God. Most Evangelicals will concede that we do, in fact, need to respond to God's grace in order for it to be effective in our lives. Even at the most basic level, Evangelicals admit that a person has to "accept Jesus." As soon as they do, you can point out that this is a form of cooperation with God. At this point, the human will and the divine will are united for the work of salvation.

This cooperation with God is not just for the individual's salvation. The New Testament makes it clear that there is more to it than that. So, for example, we affirm that Jesus is the one High Priest in the new covenant, but the New Testament also calls us to share in that priesthood (Rev. 1:5–6; 1 Pet. 2:5, 9). We do this by sharing in Christ's sufferings (Matt. 16:24; 1 Pet. 4:13). Paul calls himself a "co-worker with Christ" (1 Cor. 3:9) and says part of this is that he is crucified with Christ and shares in Christ's sufferings (2 Cor. 1:5; Phil. 3:10).

If the Evangelical believes the Bible and wants to live the Christian life, he will not only admit that he needs to cooperate with God for his own salvation, but also that this cooperation is part of a larger identification with Christ, and that this identification with Christ is for the salvation of the world. He will also admit that in some mysterious way, the sufferings we endure are part of the way God works to redeem the world.

## *Mary, Evangelist*

Once an Evangelical admits that cooperation with God is not only possible, but necessary, it opens up the idea that there is a purpose for our co-working with God. We cooperate with God for the salvation of the world. Here is another point where the Evangelical critic can connect. The Evangelical believes that each one of us has a new mission in life: We are to proclaim Christ crucified. We are to spread the gospel and share the saving work of Christ with the world. We are called to prayer, holiness, and evangelism. From there, it is a small step to see that this is another way of saying that we are called to be mediators of Christ's love and forgiveness.

Every Christian believes that he or she is called to pray for the world, to intercede and to mediate for others, to have a "ministry of reconciliation" (2 Cor. 5:18–19). Evangelicals know the Old Testament examples of Moses and Abraham interceding on behalf of others to God, and all Christians agree to the need to mediate in prayer for others. This is a good way to explain the Mediatrix role of the Blessed Virgin Mary. Mary is the first evangelist. She carried the Word of God in her body, kept it there, and bore it to the world. This was her practical role in the Incarnation, but it was also her theological role. In doing this she shows us our lesser calling to be mediators of the New Covenant and ministers of reconciliation.

It is true that Mary's role as Mediatrix is more cosmic than our own, but the principles are the same. Understanding our own share in God's saving work through mediatory prayer and sacrifice helps us understand how she does the same thing, only bigger and better, because she is the holiest of human beings and the one who is closest to the Son of God.

It is worth discussing the fact that the Fathers of the Church saw Mary as Mediator of All graces. Cyril of Alexandria in the fourth century writes,

> Hail, Mary Mother of God, venerable treasure of the whole world . . . it is you through whom the Holy Trinity is glorified and adored . . . through whom the tempter, the devil is cast down from heaven, through whom the fallen creature is raised up to heaven, through whom all creation, once imprisoned by idolatry, has reached knowledge of the truth, through whom nations are brought to repentance.[2]

Ephrem the Syrian, also writing in the fourth century, says, "With the Mediator,

---

2   Cyril of Alexandria, *Homily IV Preached at Ephesus Against Nestorius*. Quoted in Gambero, *Mary and the Fathers of the Church*, 248.

you are the Mediatrix of the entire world." And Antipater of Bostra, a father of the Council of Ephesus, wrote about the Blessed Virgin in the fifth century, "Hail, you who acceptably intercede as Mediatrix for mankind."

These quotations can be multiplied from the liturgies and theological writings of the day. The writers' exalted language shows how highly they thought of Mary's role as mediator and co-redeemer. This view of Mary as Mediatrix was not a later invention, but rather comes to us from the early Church.

The Evangelical critic may go along with you thus far, but he still finds the title "Co-Redemptrix" a stretch. Mary may have had an intimate understanding of the redemptive work of Christ, and she may have a role as intercessor and prayer warrior, but it doesn't necessarily follow that she is the Co-Redemptrix. At this point it is worth explaining that we don't suggest that Mary's cooperation with God is equal to Christ's work. It is of a different order, but it is necessary nonetheless. Mother Teresa's words "No Mary, No Jesus" express a profound truth. God chose to bring his Son into the world through the cooperation of Mary. Without that cooperation there would have been no Incarnation and therefore no Redemption.

## *Mater Dolorosa*

An Evangelical may accept this in theory, but still may find it difficult to understand how Mary can be called a "co-redemptrix." It is worthwhile going back to the mysterious words of St. Paul. In an astounding phrase, St. Paul says that his sharing in Christ's sufferings is actually effective. It completes "what is lacking in Christ's afflictions" on behalf of the Church (Col. 1:24). If he has to complete Christ's sufferings, is St. Paul implying that Christ's death on the cross was insufficient? Not at all. Instead, he is teaching that the all-sufficient sacrifice has to be completed by being preached, accepted, and embraced by our cooperation, and that our suffering plays a mysterious part in this action. In that way the Redemption of Christ is applied and brought alive in the present moment by our own cooperation in that one, full, final sacrifice. No one says we are equal to Christ. Instead, by grace, our cooperation becomes a part of Christ's all-sufficient sacrifice.

If Paul shared in a mysterious way in Christ's sufferings, and by doing so he shared in the redemptive work of the cross, then it is not too difficult to see how we are all called to do the same thing. In fact, in Romans 12, Paul exhorts us to do just that when he says, "Present your bodies as a living sacrifice" (Rom. 12:1). Jesus also tells us that we must "take up our cross and follow him if we would be his disciples" (Matt. 16:24).

If Mary was the person who was closest to Jesus, and if she was his first disciple, doesn't it follow that these truths would also apply to her? This is just what the New Testament prophesies. When Jesus was presented in the temple, the prophet Simeon, under the inspiration of the Holy Spirit, told Mary that "a sword will pierce your own heart also" (Luke 2:35). This verse is the basis for the Catholic understanding that Mary shared in the sufferings of Jesus in a mysterious way, and that her sufferings were a part of the suffering he went through.

I remember when a member of our church lost her teenage son in a car accident. The mother's grief was a terrible thing to see, and it was like a part of her had died that day. These natural examples can help others to understand why we believe Mary had an intimate relationship with the suffering of Jesus.

In Westminster Cathedral in London, a beautiful painted crucifix hangs over the central altar. On the front is a portrayal of the crucified Lord, and on the back is a portrait of Mary with a pained expression, her arms in the *orans* position of prayer. This crucifix illustrates the idea of Mary as Co-Redemptrix. Through her suffering she identified totally with her son, and by bringing him into the world, enabled the accomplishment of Redemption.

## *You Can't Just Throw Me Away!*

The Evangelical may accept Mary as vital for the Incarnation and therefore the Redemption but may wonder why we insist that she has a continuing redemptive and mediatory role. We believe this because Mary's role was not once and done. Mary did not conceive and bear Jesus, then just disappear. If her action had meaning, then it was as a continuing relationship with her Son.

Within the New Testament, Mary's cooperation with God is ongoing. As she conceived Jesus, Mary began to cooperate with the work of Redemption (Luke 1:38). She continued to do so as she bore him (Luke 2:7), and went on doing so as she interceded with him at the wedding of Cana of Galilee (John 2:3). Her work continued as she attended to him at the cross (John 19:25).

As the first Christian, she kept cooperating with grace by being present at the founding of the Church at Pentecost (Acts 1:14). She persists in this role as our Mother in heaven today (Rev. 12:17).

We believe Mary's role continues because we insist that she was not simply a neutral channel for God to come into the world. She engaged with God, and that matters. Mary was not discarded by God once her purpose was completed. Instead, her cooperation installs her into an eternal relationship with God for the salvation of the world.

There's a memorable line in a movie where a boy is breaking up with a girl, and she feels used. She cries out, "I am not a tissue! You can't just throw me away!" To have used Mary to accomplish the Incarnation and then forget about her is to treat her like a tissue. God doesn't work like that. When Catholics recognize Mary as Mediatrix and Co-Redemptrix, we acknowledge that God's work in a person's life transforms them eternally. Mary was given a new name at the Annunciation: Full of Grace. The new name indicates an ontological change. She was changed into a new person with a new role forever.

The fathers of the Second Vatican Council taught:

> [The] motherhood of Mary in the order of grace continues uninterruptedly from the consent which she loyally gave at the Annunciation and which she sustained without wavering beneath the cross, until the eternal fulfillment of all the elect. Taken up to heaven she did not lay aside this saving office but by her manifold intercession continues to bring us the gifts of eternal salvation. By her maternal charity, she cares for the brethren of her Son, who still journey on earth surrounded by dangers and difficulties, until they are led into their blessed home.[3]

Understanding Mary's role in redemption sheds light on her Son, but it also sheds light on each one of her Son's disciples. He completed in her what he wants to complete in us—total transformation into his image.

Your Evangelical brother or sister may not agree with you that the Mother of God is Mediatrix and Co-Redeemer, but the proper explanation of the titles should at least give him a new appreciation of Mary and a new appreciation of the wonders God has in store for each of his sons and daughters.

---

3   *Dogmatic Constitution on the Church*, 62

## WHERE IS MARY? IMAGES IN THE OLD TESTAMENT

I was brought up in an Evangelical home, and every Sunday our church service consisted of a long Bible study as the sermon. My favorites were when the pastor went through the Old Testament and pointed out the prophecies of Jesus which were fulfilled in the New Testament.

Some of the prophecies were very specific, such as "Behold a virgin shall conceive and bear a child, and shall call his name Emmanuel" (Isaiah 7:14) or "Out of you, Bethlehem, . . . shall come one who shall be the ruler over Israel" (Micah 5:2). But the ones I liked best were more mysterious. The pastor explained that they were "archetypes of Christ." They were mysterious images that were fulfilled in the gospels.

He explained that Jesus was "foreshadowed" through the various characters of the Old Testament stories. So, for example, David the Shepherd King points to Jesus, the Son of David who is the Good Shepherd and the King of the Jews. Moses, who taught on the mountain and provided the manna in the wilderness, points to Jesus who gave the Sermon on the Mount and gave us himself as the Bread of Heaven.

Jesus is also pictured through signs and symbols. An example was the tabernacle—that portable tent-temple in which the Israelites worshipped in the wilderness. The tabernacle and specifically the "tent of meeting" where Moses met God was fulfilled in Jesus' body when St. John says in the first chapter of his gospel that the Word was "tabernacled among us" and when Jesus says the temple which will be destroyed is his body.

The pastor pointed out many such archetypal references to Jesus and the apostles from the Old Testament, but it was only when I became a Catholic that I realized how the Old Testament is also full of archetypal references to the Blessed Virgin Mary. If we are in conversation with Protestant Christians and they complain that we "worship Mary" or say there is very little in the Bible about Mary, then we need to be ready with some answers.

## Mary, Miriam and Moses

One of the ways we see Mary in the Old Testament is in the actions and character of the various women of faith in the Old Testament. Miriam, for instance, is the sister of Moses, and the name "Mary" is a variation of the Hebrew name Miriam. Miriam was the brave young girl who took her brother and put him in a reed basket boat and hid him in the shallows of the river Nile so he would not be slaughtered by Pharaoh's soldiers. In this story Moses is a type of Jesus, and baby Moses in the reed basket is a picture of baby Jesus in the manger. Miriam carries Moses, nurtures him and keeps him safe, just as Mary kept Jesus safe from Herod's slaughter. Finally, like Mary she hands Moses over to the world so he can fulfill his destiny.

The stories of miraculous births in the Old Testament all point to Mary's role in the Incarnation. Old Sarah who was past childbearing, the mother of Samson who prayed for a son, and Hannah, the mother of the prophet Samuel—all are women who conceived naturally, but through a miraculous answer to prayer. Although Mary's conception of Jesus was of a greater order, we see her obedience and faith mirrored in the holy women of the Old Testament.

The prophecy to Eve in the Garden of Eden that she would trample the serpent's head is a sign of Mary the Victor over evil. As the second Eve, Mary's "yes" to God counters Eve's rebellion, and through her obedience, Mary overcomes the devil. Mary as the Warrior is pictured in the brave women of the Old Testament who led the Israelites in battle, Deborah and Judith, while Mary as Queen is pictured in Queen Esther and Queen Bathsheba, Queen Mother in the court of Solomon.

## Signs and Symbols of the Virgin

Where else do we see Mary in the Old Testament? In addition to the holy women who prefigure Mary, we see the Blessed Virgin reflected in signs and symbols. The fathers of the church saw in the Burning Bush a symbol of Mary, who was touched by the Holy Spirit, but whose virginity was not consumed.

The Fathers of the Eastern Orthodox tradition also saw the Blessed Virgin prefigured in the golden censer in the temple. As the censer held the red hot coal on which to burn the incense, so Mary held the fire of the Holy Spirit, and the smoke of the incense is the sweet sacrifice of Christ rising to heaven. The pot of manna in the temple also pointed to Mary, who held within her body Christ, the Bread of Heaven.

Mary was pictured as the Gate of Jerusalem because she is the door through which Jesus came into the world. Also, Jerusalem is a pointer to heaven, so she is the gate through which we come to salvation. Mary is also pictured as the Ark of the Covenant. The Ark of the Covenant was the gold-covered wooden box in which was placed the tablets of the law of Moses, together with the Manna and the miraculous rod of the high priest Aaron.

The Ark of the Covenant was a sign of the Virgin Mary because she contained the Word of God, the Bread of Heaven and the Source of Life—her son Christ the Lord. That the Ark of the Covenant is a valid symbol of the Blessed Virgin is confirmed in the New Testament in Revelation 12, where St. John has a vision of the temple of heaven and sees the Ark of the Covenant, and then he sees a "great sign in heaven" which is the woman clothed in the sun with stars around her head and the moon under her feet. This woman is the mother of the King of the nations. In other words, the Blessed Virgin Mary.

## *Mary Our Mother*

The story of God's salvation of his people is complex and beautiful. Every detail harmonizes and fits together. At the beginning we are given the story of Adam and Eve in the Garden of Eden. Then St. Paul teaches us that Jesus Christ is the second Adam. The first theologians in the church understood that Mary was therefore the second Eve.

Throughout the Old Testament, the prophecies of Christ the Lord come to us through individuals, signs and symbols. The prophecies concerning Mary his mother, along with the Apostles, the Church and the sacraments are all hidden there. St. Augustine said, "The New Testament is hidden in the Old, and the Old is made manifest in the new."

When we look more deeply into the Old Testament and study the writings of the fathers of the church, we can see how the mystery of God's salvation was woven into the stories of the Jews right from the beginning. Once we gather even a little of this information we will be equipped to share our knowledge with those who attack and misunderstand our faith.

An Answer *Not* An Argument / Fr. Dwight Longenecker

# HOLY MARY, MOTHER OF GOD

> I have long recognized the unique vocation of Our Lady, called to the highest honor among all created beings. It is a fact of history that, if true honor is not paid to her as the Mother of God, people put our Lord in her place as the highest of creation rather than adoring him as God Incarnate.
>
> —Rt. Rev. Mgr. Graham Leonard, *The Path to Rome*[1]

The former Anglican Bishop of London—later ordained as a Catholic priest—sums up the reasoning for the church's most ancient title for the Blessed Virgin Mary. Put simply, Mary's title of Mother of God insures Christ's true place as the unique Son of God and Son of Man.

The title "Theotokos," which literally means God-bearer, was the title given to Mary by the Greek fathers starting with Origen in the early third century. Some even think it can be traced to Hippolytus, who died in the year 236. This term for the Virgin Mary was used increasingly by the early Church, but in the early fifth century, it was attacked by the heretic Nestorius, who wanted to replace the term Theotokos with *Christotokos* or "Christ-bearer." Nestorius, in a sincere attempt to avoid an earlier heresy called Apollinarianism, asserted that there were two separate persons conjoined in Jesus Christ. Thus, the Blessed Virgin Mary in giving Jesus human flesh could be the "Christ-bearer" but not "God bearer."

Nestorius was opposed by St. Cyril of Alexandria, and the controversy was referred to a Council of Rome in the year 430. Pope Celestine condemned Nestorius' teaching, and in the meantime the emperor arranged a General Council to meet at Ephesus. It met in the summer of 431 and condemned Nestorius, therefore reaffirming the already ancient title Theotokos. What is clear from the controversy surrounding Nestorius is that the title Theotokos is not primarily an exaltation of the Blessed Virgin Mary, but a defense of orthodox Christology. The Council of Ephesus upheld a fully orthodox view of Jesus, and to do this they reaffirmed the devotion to the Blessed Virgin Mary,

---

1 Appearing in Dwight Longenecker, ed., *The Path to Rome: Modern Journeys to the Catholic Church* (Gracewing Publishing, 1999), 31.

which in turn supported the fullest understanding of Christ's divinity.

Just twenty years after the Council of Ephesus, another council was held, this time in the city of Chalcedon. On 8 October 451 the council opened and dealt with another heresy called Eutychianism. As a result of the council, the Definition of Chalcedon was drawn up. This definition reaffirmed the basic definition of Christ's divinity given at the Council of Nicaea in 325. It expressly repudiated those who deny the title Theotokos for the Blessed Virgin Mary and went on to reassert the orthodox position that Our Lord was "One Person in Two Natures which are united unconfusedly, unchangeably indivisibly inseparably."

I have gone into a bit of detail about the events of the fifth century for a specific reason. One of the things which draws all Christians together is the fact that all who call themselves orthodox look to these first councils of the church for their definition of true belief about the united manhood and divinity of Jesus Christ. The Definition of Chalcedon, based on the earlier definitions of Ephesus and Nicaea, is looked to as a test of orthodoxy not only by the Catholic Church and most of the Eastern Churches, but also by Protestant believers. However, if Protestants claim that their orthodoxy stems from these early councils, there is a problem.

The Council of Ephesus specifically upheld the title of Theotokos for the Blessed Virgin Mary, and the Council of Chalcedon expressly repudiated those who would deny Mary that title. Therefore, those modern-day Christians who deny Mary the title of Theotokos are actually condemned by the very councils to which they look for support. One might argue that the title Theotokos was affirmed by the councils as a separate measure, but it wasn't. It was affirmed as an integral part of their defense of orthodox Christology. The historical record shows that devotion to the Blessed Virgin Mary as the Mother of God developed at the same time as the orthodox understanding of Jesus as the God-Man. Graham Leonard's pithy statement explains why the two beliefs developed together. As Jesus came to be understood as God incarnate, it became clear that Mary, as his human mother, must have been specially preserved from sin by God. This special purity made her the highest of created beings. Devotion to her was therefore totally intertwined with submission and obedience to her Son, the incarnate God.

This unity of man and woman is hinted at in the Scriptures' doctrine of marriage. From Genesis through to the teachings of Our Lord in the gospels and the teachings of St. Paul, man and woman are said to be "one flesh." In 1 Corinthians Paul reaffirms the unity that exists between man and woman (1 Cor. 11:8–12):

> For man was not made from woman, but woman from man. Neither was man created for woman, but woman for man. . . . Nevertheless, in the Lord woman is not independent of man nor man of woman; for as woman was made from man, so man is now born of woman. And all things are from God.

In the divine economy, man and woman are interdependent and in the mystery of the redemption, God chose for both Jesus and his mother to play interdependent roles.

There are some non-Catholics who would therefore grant Mary the title of Theotokos for theological reasons, but they still do not practice any form of Marian devotion. This is illogical and truncated because in every other aspect of our faith, our worship, devotion and adoration are inspired and united to the doctrines we profess. How can one grant Mary the title "Mother of God" and yet refrain from using the ancient prayer in which we say, "Holy Mary, Mother of God, pray for us now and in the hour of our death"?

Worship of Jesus Christ as "God from God, Light from Light, True God from True God, begotten, not made, consubstantial with the Father" is therefore a unity with prayerful devotion to his mother. With her and through her we affirm and bow before the one who is God made man. Those who deny Marian devotion sometimes sincerely object because they believe devotion to Mary detracts from proper worship of her Son. But this is to misunderstand the Church's teaching and practice. Devotion to the Blessed Virgin is constantly united with the worship of her Son. "Woman is not independent of man nor man of woman" (1Cor. 11:11). This unity of belief and practice cannot be separated, and just as the early church taught, those who deny that Mary is Theotokos also impugn the true divinity of her Son—even if they are sincerely unaware that they are doing so.

The famous convert Kimberly Hahn has said, "There are three things that keep evangelicals away from the Catholic Church—Mary, Mary and Mary." While it is true that evangelicals have a strong resistance to Marian devotion, Catholics should not apologize or back away from the issue. Instead, it should be shown that devotion to the Blessed Virgin Mary has been an integral part of orthodox Christianity from the very earliest days of the Church. It should be pointed out that the early Church fathers actually considered a proper view of Christ to be dependent on the proper understanding of Mary's identity. Furthermore, those who object to Catholic practice should be reminded that the vast majority of Christians down through the ages and around the world today incorporate the Marian dimension into their Christian lives in a daily loving devotion. Most importantly, it should be stressed that devotion to Mary is not something different than their already keen love for Christ; instead, devotion to the Mother of God is a fuller experience of His everlasting love.

# MOTHER OF GOD OR MOTHER GODDESS?

I can remember my shock when as an Evangelical student, I heard a German Catholic friend refer to Mary as "*Gottesmutter*." The phrase means, "Mother of God," but in my ignorance of the German language I thought he was calling Mary, "Goddess Mother." It confirmed my suspicion that Catholics worshipped Mary as the Mother Goddess. It turned out I was wrong—not only about the German language, but about Catholic beliefs regarding Mary, the Mother of God.

The charge that Catholics worship Mary as some sort of Mother Goddess comes not only from Evangelical Protestants. An increasing number of "new atheists" also go to great lengths to reveal the supposed links between the Christian faith and ancient pagan religions. They link Baptism to Mithraism and show how the doctrine of the incarnation has its roots in pagan god-man myths. They like to reveal how the Resurrection and the Virgin Birth and the Ascension are all just rehashed ideas from pagan religions the world over. One of the favorite lines of attack is directed to the Catholic devotion to the Blessed Virgin Mary.

At first glance, the argument seems convincing. Check out the images of Isis on the Internet and you'll find a Madonna and Child that seems identical to typical Catholic images of the Virgin and child. In ancient Egypt, Isis was known as the "Divine Mother" or the "Queen of Heaven." As a virgin she gave birth to Horus, the sun god. It was Horus who killed Typhon, the Egyptian version of the devil, and it was claimed that Isis remained a virgin forever.

Critics of Catholicism go on to notice that virtually every primitive society had some sort of Mother Goddess, and they charge Catholics for being pagan because we call Mary our Mother, the Queen of Heaven, the Mother of God, and load her with a cult like "worship." "I can never," said the Anglo-Irish Protestant Rev. M. Hobart Seymour, in his *Evenings with the Romanists*, "forget the shock I received when I first saw in their churches in Italy, the Virgin Mary crowned as Queen of heaven, seated on the same throne with Jesus crowned King of heaven. They were the God-man and God-woman enthroned alike.... There was nothing to distinguish the one above the other."[1] It's an understandable misconception, and the whole topic is very intriguing, so it's worth taking a more detailed look.

## *Mary and the Bible Christian*

First, we need to stop and examine the criticisms of Evangelical Protestants. They accuse Catholics of being pagan, because they believe veneration of the Blessed Virgin must have been adopted from paganism unthinkingly. There are several problems with this theory, though.

First of all, when you examine the pagan mother goddesses, the differences between them and the Virgin Mary are actually more outstanding than their similarities. For example, very few of the ancient mother goddesses purport to be virgins. There are mother goddesses and virgin goddesses, but very few virgin mother goddesses. The critic of Catholicism might see "Statue of goddess" and "statue of Mary" and equate them, but on closer examination, while there are echoes and similarities, the pagan goddesses are not essentially like the Catholic understanding of Mary at all.

The pagan mother goddesses are not like Mary because they originate in a completely different way. The pagan goddesses are the result of centuries of religious myth developing within a pagan culture. The gods and goddesses were always mythical figures. They were characters in fanciful fables that carried great meaning.

Mary of Nazareth, on the other hand, is a simple peasant girl who was touched by God and gave her consent to be the mother of the Lord. Mary may have been assumed into heaven, but she didn't start there. She started in a little house in a humble village in a backwater of the Roman Empire.

Secondly, the Evangelical critic of the Catholic Church will claim that Catholic beliefs about Mary were imported from paganism because there seems to be a symbolic link between a goddess like Isis and the Blessed Virgin Mary. Catholic devotion to Mary is therefore compromised. "Paganism," they argue, "has crept in and infected the pure Christian faith of the Bible." This is guilt by association. This form of argument is specious. A belief or practice

---

[1] Michael Hobart Seymour, *Evenings with the Romanists* (H. Hooker, 1855), 178.

must be evaluated on its own terms. The question is, "Is it true or false?" not "Is it associated with paganism?" Guilt by association would condemn the Evangelical as well, because the very beliefs he holds dear can also be shown to have "associations" with paganism.

The Evangelical Protestant may not wish to call the Blessed Virgin the "Queen of Heaven," but he does want to uphold the Virgin Birth, and the fact that Jesus was the Son of God who destroyed Satan. If guilt by association is a sound argument, then the Evangelical must give account for his beliefs, because Isis also gave birth as a virgin and her son Horus was the Son of God who defeated the devil. If the Catholic's "Queen of Heaven" was inspired by pagan Egyptian religion, then so is the Evangelical's belief in the Virgin Birth and Jesus the Son of God's victory over Satan.

Finally, the Evangelical argument blaming Catholic devotion to Mary for being pagan is undermined by the very facts of the incarnation and the gospel story. The concept of Mary as Universal Mother is not borrowed from paganism. It comes instead from a totally different, unique and obvious source. The early Christians saw Mary as their Mother because Jesus said she was.

When Christ on the cross says to the Apostle John, "Behold your Mother," he gives Mary to the whole church. This is the origin of the Catholic belief that Mary is our Mother, and this is amplified by the theology of the early church. The apostolic fathers. Irenaeus and Justin Martyr first explained that Mary was the second Eve. Mary's universal motherhood therefore springs not from some half-baked pagan smash-and-grab exercise, but from the gospel account of the crucifixion and from the Jewish context of the early Church.

## *Mary and the New Atheist*

The Evangelical Protestant objects to Catholic devotion to the Blessed Virgin Mary because he believes it to be pagan. Paganism is bad, so therefore the Catholic devotion to the Blessed Virgin must be bad. The new atheist also objects to Catholic devotions to the Blessed Virgin Mary because he thinks them pagan, and paganism is bad, so Catholic devotion to the Blessed Virgin must be bad. However, while the atheist and the Protestant object to Catholic devotion to the Blessed Virgin for the same reason, their opinions of paganism are different.

The Evangelical Protestant objects to paganism because he believes it is a religion that worships the devil. The atheist objects to paganism in the way that he objects to all religion: because it is nonsense. In equating Marian devotion to paganism, the new atheist tries to portray it as a load of Primitivistic bunkum—on the same level as belief in the tooth fairy, Santa Claus and magic spells. At best, he sees Marian devotion as a form of subconscious wish fulfillment. This is the "psychological explanation" for Marian devotion. It runs like this: "All of us participate in the collective unconscious. This is a vast realm of our human experience which is uncharted, mysterious and profound. Out of the deep surging emotion of human experience, we all share a deep longing for unity with the Mother and Father. Through religion we therefore produce a 'Super Mother' and a 'Super Father' for ourselves who we believe will fulfill all our needs and lead us at last to a heavenly home where we can live as a family happily ever after." Pagan religions produced mother goddesses in every culture, and Catholics, the psychology-driven atheist would argue, "have perhaps unconsciously made the mother of a wandering rabbi in the first century into the same sort of Super Mother figure to fulfill their deepest needs."

The explanation seems plausible. Like most psychological explanations, it has a certain sweet reasonableness to it. The only problem is that this is not the way devotion to the Blessed Virgin Mary developed. We don't have full-blown pagan-style myths of Mary, the Mother Goddess, springing up in the early church. Instead there is comparatively little mention of her in the New Testament, and where she is mentioned she is very humble, accepting and ordinary. The *Protoevangelium of James* is an early second century writing from the church in Jerusalem. In this story we are told of the Blessed Virgin's ordinary Jewish upbringing. No god and goddesses and magical mythical tales—just an ordinary girl caught up in extraordinary events.

Indeed, the New Testament records and the writings of the early church fathers show that the first Christians, rather than absorbing and adopting the pagan religions, were firm in their resistance to paganism. The early Christians endured deprivation, prison, torture and martyrdom rather than compromise the faith and give even one little pinch of incense to the pagan gods. Are we to believe that what they were really doing was adding in every bit of paganism possible? That while their friends were being tortured and killed for their resistance to paganism the early Christians were saying, "I know! Everybody really likes this Artemis goddess. Let's make Mary like her so more people will convert!" Hardly.

The atheist will reply, "It all happened much later, after the fourth century, once Christianity became the religion of the Roman Empire." However, the documents simply don't show this to be true. Rather than adopting pagan customs and beliefs, the early Christians were keen to show how the Christian faith was different from the paganism around them.

So Origen writing in the third century was careful to distinguish the virgin birth from the fable of Plato's virgin birth.[2] Furthermore, the Christians of the fourth, fifth and sixth centuries continued to weed out heresy and would not tolerate even the slightest hint of pagan practice and belief. The writers of those centuries were passionate about the correct understanding of the incarnation of Christ, and the Marian doctrine at this time developed not from a wish (conscious or not) to import paganism, but from the church's understanding of who Christ really was.

A simple reading of the Fathers of the Church shows that veneration of Mary developed simply from the seeds of her universal Motherhood given by Christ at the cross, and from the earlier concept of Mary as second Eve. The book *Mary and the Fathers of the Church*[3] by Luigi Gambero clarifies just how and when the Catholic devotion to Mary developed, and there's not a jot of paganism within it.

The climax of this early development of Marian thought comes with the definition of Mary as Mother of God or Theotokos. This title was granted to Mary at the Council of Ephesus in 431. It was not granted as some glorious honor to Mary as some sort of pagan Queen of Heaven, but as a theological term clarifying her relationship to her son and therefore affirming his full divinity. This was done, not to promote some strange and lavish pagan ritual, and not through some careless infection of the faith by paganism, but as a result of careful thought, debate and resolution of belief.

---

2   Origen, *Against Celsus* Book 1, Ch. 37.

3   Luigi S. M. Gambero, *Mary and the Fathers of the Church: The Blessed Virgin Mary in Patristic Thought* (San Francisco: Ignatius Press, 2006).

## *Pagan Mary?*

Nevertheless, the Protestant and the atheist critics of Marian devotion do raise an intriguing question, and it is not sufficient to merely dismiss their criticism as crude anti-Catholicism. In fact, there is a relationship between Christianity and paganism. There has to be, because Christianity developed within a context of an ancient pagan culture. Therefore, to answer the Protestant and atheist critics satisfactorily, we must be able to explain the true relationship between ancient pagan religions and the Christian faith.

Firstly, while it is true that the early Christians went to their deaths to repudiate paganism, it is also true that the early Christian apologists—including St. John and St. Paul writing in the New Testament—were willing to use pagan ideas and philosophical concepts to communicate the gospel. As all good missionaries do, they found connecting points with the culture, philosophy and religion of their audience. So, for example, St. John uses the Greek philosophical term *"logos"* to explain the incarnation. In Athens St. Paul takes the idea of the "unknown God" and preaches the gospel of Jesus Christ to his hearers. St. Paul adopts the concept of "mystery" prevalent in the mystery religions, while the writer to the Hebrews employs Platonist ideas in his discussion of an earthly and heavenly temple.

Likewise, the early Christians used existing religious and philosophical concepts to communicate the reality of Jesus Christ. They had to, because that was the language of their culture. They used the concepts of their culture, but as they did so, they transformed those ideas from the inside out. For St. John, the mysterious *logos* is no longer mysterious, for it has taken human flesh. For St. Paul, the "mystery hidden for ages and ages" (Col. 1:26) is now fully revealed in Christ Jesus. Time and again, the writers of the New Testament and the first theologians of the church take an existing concept or idea and use it to explain the full reality of the gospel of Jesus Christ.

It is therefore true that creative links exist between the pagan culture of the day and the religion of the early church. It only remains to ask why this might be, and whether it is good or bad. To answer that question, we turn to Galatians 4:4: "In the fullness of time God sent forth his Son, born of a woman, born under the law." By this St. Paul means that the incarnation of Christ happened at the time and the place, in the culture and in the context that God intended. It was no mistake that Christ Jesus came into a world replete with numerous pagan religions, philosophies and beliefs.

It is also no mistake that he did so through the Hebrew race and religion. From the beginning, the Jews lived as a unique people within a surrounding pagan culture. From within their culture and context God used them to correct the pagan culture and context. From the start, their witness was of one loving God the Father who revealed himself to his people through the nitty gritty of human history and through the tender complexity of the human race. For Christ to have been born in the heart of the Middle East, in the heart of the Roman Empire, in the heart of a whole array of pagan religions, Eastern philosophies and a virtual smorgasbord of religious choices, was not a mistake. From within this swirl of religions Christianity was formed, grew and was formulated by God's inspiration. The Christians were influenced by the surrounding religions and philosophies, but where such influence occurred, the new Christian faith corrected and fulfilled the existing religions and philosophies.

C. S. Lewis summed it up when he was talking with J. R. R. Tolkien about the power of myth. Lewis had observed that the Christian myth was like all the other myths in the sense that myths were "lies." Tolkien disagreed. When Lewis then asked Tolkien whether "the story of Christ is simply a true myth, a myth working on us in the same way as the others, but a myth that really happened," Tolkien's answer was "Yes."[4]

Within this view, we see all the pagan religions, all the pagan philosophies, all the pagan myths and stories as pointers to the coming truth. The pagan Mother goddesses, therefore, were hints and guesses of the true Mother of God and Queen of Heaven. They were imperfect pointers and foreshadowings of the young Jewish girl from Nazareth from whom God would be born, and who therefore is rightly called the Mother of God, the Mother of the Church, and the Mother of all the Baptized.

---

4    The event is recounted in Lewis's *Letter to Arthur Greeves, 31 October, 1931*.

# *Conclusion*

## ALL THAT CATHOLIC STUFF IS CONNECTED

A priest friend said one winter the Methodist minister knocked on the rectory door with a question. He was an eager young minister, ready to learn and adopt new practices where they might be helpful. Once he had come into the rectory he said, "Father, I have a question."

"Yes? How can I help?"

"Well, Ash Wednesday is coming up and I'm wondering where you Catholics get those ashes you use."

"Why do you ask?"

"Well, last year I wanted to, you know, put ashes on everybody's foreheads for Ash Wednesday so I got some ashes from my fireplace and added some water and it was a terrible mess!"

My priest friend chuckled, "It would be! We get our ashes for Ash Wednesday from a special service the night before. We save the palms from the Palm Sunday from the previous year and we burn them in a little brazier with special prayers. Then we use those ashes—which are very pure and fine—for Ash Wednesday."

The Methodist was delighted, "Gosh!" He enthused, "All this Catholic stuff is connected!"

He was right about that, and the longer I am a Catholic the more I realize that all this Catholic stuff is indeed connected.

What we believe about marriage, for example, is connected with what we believe about the identity of male and female, and what we believe about men and women connects with what happened in the Garden of Eden, and what happened in the Garden of Eden connects with what happened when the Angel Gabriel came to Mary and what happened there connects with Jesus Christ the second Adam and that connects with his death and resurrection and the forgiveness of humanity and the end of all things and the beginning of a new world.

It is the same with everything in the Catholic universe. Canon Law is connected with the liturgy, which is connected with our prayer life, which interlinks with our doctrines, which inform our actions which connect with politics, economics, environmentalism and everything else.

This is one of the ways in which Catholic means "Universal". It touches all things and connects all things. It is the big system that excludes nothing. All of human history is here—the tragedies and the triumphs. All of human accomplishments in art, architecture, music, science, philosophy, literature, languages and more.

If you are exploring the Catholic world, your exploration, in one sense will never end. But in another sense, it does end, for what we learn is a kind of remembering, and our exploration ends in a homecoming.

## *About the Author*

Fr Dwight Longenecker was brought up in an Evangelical home. After graduating from Bob Jones University he studied theology at Oxford University and was ordained as an Anglican minister. He served as a curate, a school chaplain at Cambridge and as a country vicar on the Isle of Wight. In 1995, with his family, he was received into the Catholic Church.

In 2006 he and his family returned to his native USA and he was ordained as a Catholic priest under the special pastoral provision for married former Protestant ministers. He now serves as the Pastor of Our Lady of the Rosary Church in Greenville, South Carolina.

A popular speaker at conferences and parish missions, Fr Longenecker has written over twenty books and booklets about Catholic faith and culture as well as thousands of articles for numerous journals, papers, magazines and websites. Read his award winning blog, *Standing on My Head*, listen to his podcasts, browse his books and be in touch at **DwightLongenecker.com**.

# *Books by the Author*

Available from **DwightLongenecker.com**

### Mystery of the Magi

*The Quest to Identify the Three Wise Men*

Who were the magi who came to visit the Christ child? Skeptics dismiss the story as a pious fairy tale. Believers hold to an elaborate tale of mystery and wonder. Fr Longenecker cuts through the legend and discovers who the wise men were, where they came from and why they made the journey to Bethlehem.

"Longenecker's Magi are no longer exotic kings from distant lands; they are real figures, the pieces missing from many ancient puzzles."

—Dr Margaret Barker is a former President of the Society for Old Testament Study and co- founder of the Temple Studies Group.

"The book is aimed at readers with no prior knowledge of the Bible and also at biblical scholars. I believe it succeeds admirably for both audiences. In addition, it is a mine of useful information about the Middle East at the time of Christ. It is the best book I know about the Magi and throws new light upon the birth narratives in the gospels. Buy it as a present for others or for yourself!"

—Sir Colin Humphreys CBE, Author, *The Mystery of the Last Supper*

# Our Lady?
*A Catholic/Evangelical Debate*

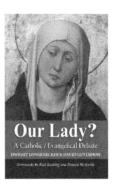

Converts to the Catholic faith usually find Catholic beliefs about the Mother of Jesus to be a huge stumbling block. Fr Longenecker got together with an old Bob Jones University classmate to discuss the matter. David Gustafson and Dwight Longenecker wrestle over the Scriptural statements and traditions surrounding Mary of Nazareth.

"There is simply no other book in print that explores this most immovable impasse between Protestants and Catholics in a way that both uncompromising Evangelicals and Catholics can wholly applaud. Clear, honest, mutually respectful uncompromising and illuminating."

—Peter Kreeft

"In this book the contention is good-natured, even winsome. The writers are frank with one another and with their readers. They acknowledge their own re-thinkings, their own unsureness, their own strong attachments to the Christian faith. In many things they are in full agreement; in many not. Even with respect to Mary they agree on much, but their disagreements are many and are not trivial. Each represents his position well and cordially. These are men you would be willing to take a transcontinental road trip with, with no fear of boredom or claustrophobic annoyance."

—Karl Keating, Foreword to *Our Lady?*

# St Benedict and St Thérèse

*The Little Rule and the Little Way*

St Benedict stands for the wisdom of age. St Thérèse for the wisdom of innocence. Fr Longenecker discusses the lives and writings of these favorite saints in a book that has become a classic.

"I encourage you to read this book slowly and so follow Father Longenecker as he leads through different aspects of the spiritual life with this innocent little girl and wise patriarch. Through a few Chestertonian-type paradoxes, Fr Longenecker will open our eyes, ears and hearts so we can listen to *St. Benedict and St. Thérèse*, and follow them as they show us the way back to God."

—From the foreword by Fr Francis Bethel, OSB of Clear Creek Monastery

"*St Benedict and St Thérèse* is a wonderful book and will be of profit to a wide readership. The insights are theologically sound, spiritually illuminating, and expressed with such down-to earth simplicity and delightful humour that, without even noticing, readers will be disarmed and drawn into great mysteries."

—Fr John Saward, Author of *The Way of the Lamb*

# The Gargoyle Code

*A Screwtape Letters volume for Lent*

*The Gargoyle Code* is a collection of email correspondence between Senior devil Slubgrip and trainee devil Dogwart. The letters instruct Dogwart how to tempt his young Catholic victim, err, I mean patient. Meanwhile Slubgrip has to keep an eye on his own, elderly Catholic patient all the time watching his back because the other devils are plotting his downfall. *The Gargoyle Code* provides a hilarious and sobering journey through Lent for serious Catholics who are not always so serious.

Reviewers write:

"This was just as good as *The Screwtape Letters*. Fr. Longenecker kept within the same style as CS Lewis and the humor was there on every page. It was written for a Lenten read with a letter a day during Lent, but I confess that I read it like a book and enjoyed it just as much."

"I really enjoyed this book and was very impressed. I have read *"The Screwtape Letters"* by C.S. Lewis and it was a great book, but this book I believe is better. With the world the way it is today, this book really makes you think about the little things....Well worth buying and I have recommended this book to everyone I talk to."

# Slubgrip Instructs
*Fifty Days with the Devil*

Having been betrayed and sent down, Slubgrip now finds himself sentenced to teach Popular Culture 101 at Bowelbages University. His lectures and meetings, and those of his collection of fiendish guest lecturers are recorded by the security division at Bowelbages and the transcripts comprise the manuscript of *Slubgrip Instructs*.

Slubgrip's lectures take the reader through the whole range of the temptations in popular culture that undermine the Catholic faith.

While busy teaching and bullying his students, Slubgrip has his eye on toppling President Thornblade and his old enemies–Commissioner Crasston and head of Detention, the tempter Snozzle. Will Slubgrip's coup succeed or will he receive yet another "invitation to dinner down below?"

Reviewers write:

"Great read. A old modern understanding of the *Screwtape letters*."

"*Slubgrip Instructs: Fifty Days with the Devil*, while a sequel to Longenecker's *Gargoyle Code*, stands alone and does the 'make you think twice about everything in your life' job quite nicely."

"It's a fast read if you sit down to read it, but I would encourage you to take your copy (because, I assure you, you need one!) and savor it. Consider what's written and how popular culture is truly impacting you. It's not an easy truth to face."

# Catholicism Pure and Simple

*Catholicism Pure and Simple* begins with arguments for the existence of God and moves through the story of Jesus Christ, the work of the Holy Spirit, and moves on to discuss the church, sacraments, prayer, and the Catholic life.

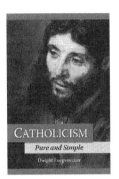

*Catholicism Pure and Simple* is written in a straightforward style without complicated theological references, liturgical terms or high brow cultural or historical terminology. Excellent as a text book for confirmation candidates, RCIA members, and all those searching for a beginners understanding of the Catholic faith.

"Father Dwight Longenecker does for Catholicism what C. S. Lewis did for "mere Christianity". Those looking for the way home by taking the path to Rome will find this book an excellent and reliable guide for the journey."

— Joseph Pearce, Author of *C.S.Lewis and the Catholic Church*

"Convert Father Dwight makes a powerfully "pure and simple" presentation of the Catholic faith. From fundamentalist Protestant to Anglican to Catholic; from America to England and back again; he asked difficult questions, and in this fine text, he successfully presents the answers that helped him make his journey home."

—Marcus Grodi, host EWTN's Journey's Home, Author of *How Firm a Foundation* and *Pillar and Bulwark*

Made in the USA
Columbia, SC
13 May 2019